Alexander Wilmot

The Poetry of South Africa

Collected and Arranged

Alexander Wilmot

The Poetry of South Africa
Collected and Arranged

ISBN/EAN: 9783744751803

Printed in Europe, USA, Canada, Australia, Japan

Cover: Foto ©Thomas Meinert / pixelio.de

More available books at **www.hansebooks.com**

THE POETRY

OF

SOUTH AFRICA

COLLECTED AND ARRANGED

BY

A. WILMOT

LONDON
SAMPSON LOW, MARSTON, SEARLE, & RIVINGTON
CAPE TOWN
J. C. JUTA & CO.
1887

PREFACE.

THIS collection of verse has been made from various sources in the Cape Colony, Natal, and the Transvaal, and it is a matter of regret that many pieces of interest have been omitted owing to the difficulty of obtaining copies. Also as most colonists in South Africa understand the Dutch language "as spoken there," it could be wished that certain well-known productions in the "Boerentaal" could have been preserved in these pages. Some of the inimitable "versions" of Reitz,—for instance, his rendering of "Tam o' Shanter" and "The Maid of Athens," and some others which have appeared from time to time, we believe, in one of the Cape journals, ought not to be forgotten.

We have received from Natal, since this volume was "in the press," some lines by the late T. Fannin, who used in the olden days to sing his own rhymes in right good style. We do not apologise to our readers for giving these in their entirety.

"THE SMOUSE."

"I'm a Smouse, I'm a Smouse in the wilderness wide—
The veld is my home, and the wagon's my pride;
The crack of my "voerslag" shall sound o'er the lea,.
I'm a Smouse, I'm a Smouse, and the trader is free!
I heed not the Governor, I fear not his law,
I care not for 'civilisation' (?) one straw—
And ne'er to 'Ompanda'—'Umgazis' I'll throw,
While my arm carries fist, or my foot bears a toe!
'Trek,' 'trek,' ply the whip,—touch the fore oxen's skin,
I'll warrant we'll 'go it' through thick and through thin—
'Loop! loop ye oud skellums! ot Vigmaan trek jy.'
I'm a Smouse, I'm a Smouse, and the trader is free!

They may talk of quick going by mail or by rail—
What matters? our wagon creeps on like a snail;
What to 'her' is the steam-engine's whistle and din?
We have time all before, and the 'prog' all within—
The snows of Kathlamba our progress can't stay;
We mount to its summit, and travel away,
Or go we by Biggarsberg—wagon upset,
The tent lies in atoms, the stuff is all wet—
Never mind, that won't hurt us—we'll soon get it dry.
But ho! there go Elands—saddle up, boys! mount! fly!
Load your rifles, give chase as they bound o'er the lea—
I m a Smouse, I'm a Smouse, and the trader is free!

I'm alone—I'm alone, and 'tis night on the plain—
And I think, as I lie, of old England again;
The jackal cries round me, the wolf quits his lair,
And the roar of the lion resounds through the air—
'Alamagtig!' cries Jansi—'Ma-wo!' cries Kewitt;
The cattle stand trembling—the Smouse on his feet.

> My 'Lancaster' rings, while the brute gives a bound,
> And the king of the desert lies dead on the ground!
> Hurrah! then, what care I for king or for prince?
> My horse and my gun are my pride and defence;
> The town for the coward—the desert for me!
> I'm a Smouse, I'm a Smouse, and the trader is free!"

All is changed since these lines were written, and since Pringle (the "father" of South African verse) "sang" amid the wild surroundings of his home. The whistle of the locomotive has taken the place of the shrill cry of the Kaffir. The lion has retired from business. The "big game" which used to cover the plains beyond the Drachensberg has gone, never to return; and the wandering trader has to pay taxes, and is no longer in need of a gun. The railway from Delagoa Bay to the Portuguese border is almost completed. Soon "excursions to Ophir" will be advertised, and the romance of the "Dark Continent" will be dead! There is little time for thought or rest in a country which can show a town risen up, as by Aladdin's power, in a few short months, holding five thousand people, all gathered together for one object—gold.* Still, and in spite of all this, we hope our modest volume may not be wholly neglected, but will find a welcome in many a home. There must be "intervals for refreshment," however transient, both for body and mind, even in a world where the "go as you please"

---

* Johannésberg.

race for wealth engages everybody, and we trust that many colonists will find something in these pages to satisfy their tastes even if it be only a reminder of the days when their fathers were young, and ventured over the sea to make for themselves homes in untrodden wilds.

B.

24th September 1887.

CONTENTS.

		PAGE
A Christmas Apparition	*Cole*	166
Afar in the Desert	*Pringle*	10
Afric's Greeting	*Bidwell*	240
After a Storm	*Watermeyer*	120
Ammap and Griet	*S. A. M.*	120
Angel's Message (The)	*Bidwell*	249
Baron's Adventure	*Brodrick*	226
Beautiful Island of Dreams	*Wilmot*	114
Bechuana Boy	*Pringle*	4
Before Ulundi	*Brodrick*	225
Be Kind to One Another	*Bidwell*	260
Better Land (The)	*Brodrick*	231
Brown Hunter's Song	*Pringle*	30
Burghers' Gathering (The)	*Impey*	187
Bushman (Song of the Wild)	*Pringle*	25
Bushman (The)	,,	31
Caffer (The)	,,	32
Caffer Commando	,,	42
Cape of Good Hope	*Thomson*	115
Cape of Good Hope	*Selwyn*	272
Cape of Storms	*Pringle*	31
Captive of Camalu	,,	27
Change	*Ochse*	209
Churl of the Period	*Bidwell*	252

CONTENTS.

		PAGE
Colours of the 1st-24th	*Dugmore*	91
Contentment	*Ochse*	203
Coranna (The)	*Pringle*	24
Courtship (South African)	*Brodrick*	227
Dear Old Land (The)	*Dugmore*	55
Defenders of Glen Lynden	,,	89
Desolate Valley (The)	*Pringle*	22
Diamond Digger (The)	*Bidwell*	242
Dives Redivivus	*Cruikshanks*	186
"Dolly" (A Remembrance)	*Brodrick*	232
Drink	*Wilmot*	110
Drunkard's Child (The)	*Bidwell*	245
Emigrants (The)	*Pringle*	1
Emigrant's Cabin	,,	48
Epitaph on a Diamond Digger	*Brodrick*	239
Erythrina Tree (The)	*M. E. Barber*	274
Evening Rambles	*Pringle*	13
Eveleen	*C. P. M.*	126
Ezekiel xlvii.	*Ochse*	207
Faded Photograph (The)	*Longmore*	124
Farewell to English Friends	*Dugmore*	66
Farewell to Madeira	*Stirling*	128
Farewell to Fifty-five	*Selwyn*	130
Flight of the "Amakosa"	*Cole*	146
Forester of the Neutral Ground	*Pringle*	44
Freedom's Home	*G. L.*	172
Funeral in the Abbey	*Dugmore*	59
Ghona Widow's Lullaby	*Pringle*	33
Going Home	*Brodrick*	234
Good Hope	*Thomson*	117
Graaff Reinet (To)	*Selwyn*	136
Heavenly Friendship	*Ochse*	210

CONTENTS.

		PAGE
Horace (Ode from)	*Watermeyer*	118
Hottentot (The)	*Pringle*	32
Idyl of a Prince	*Cole*	154
Incantation (The)	*Pringle*	40
In the Drought Lands	*Wilmot*	100
In Memoriam (Gordon)	*Brown*	238
In Memoriam (Templeton)	*Selwyn*	268
Kosa (The)	*Pringle*	36
Lament on the Gutter, P. Elizabeth	*Selwyn*	139
Landing of British Settlers, 1820	*Wilmot*	101
Last of the Bowkers	*Bidwell*	244
"Lead, Kindly Light"	*Selwyn*	133
Lines in an Album	*Ochse*	211
Lion and Giraffe	*Pringle*	20
Lion Hunt	,,	18
"Lord, what is Man?"	*Selwyn*	269
Makanna's Gathering	*Pringle*	38
Mankoraan (in the Country of)	*Wilmot*	109
Mission of the Sails	*Adamastor*	237
Missionary's Farewell	*Dugmore*	67
Morning Wish for a Friend	,,	85
Natal Diggings	*Moodie*	191
Nature	,,	192
"Not Here"	*Ochse*	204
Night Thought	*Dugmore*	86
Our Boys	,,	95
Oxford Bible	*Marie*	235
Ox Waggon (Rhyme of the)	*Selwyn*	270
Paddy's Love Symptoms	*Bidwell*	261
Past and Present	*Dugmore*	75
Platteklip Cascade	*B.*	265
Porter, Hon. W.	*Cruikshanks*	178

CONTENTS.

		PAGE
Port Elizabeth Pyramid	*Selwyn*	266
Proverbial Philosophy	*Bidwell*	262
Precepts for Young and Old	,,	257
Reminiscence, 1820	*Dugmore*	72
Revelation xxii.	*Ochse*	205
Robert Godlington	*Bidwell*	241
Rock of Reconcilement	*Pringle*	43
Romance from the "Fields"	*Overton*	142
"Rorke's Drift"	*Mitford*	212
"Rorke's Drift"	*Brodrick*	223
Sails (The Worn Out)	*E. L. B.*	237
"Salted" Steed	*Brodrick*	141
Settlers' Jubilee (The)	*Cruikshanks*	181
Shell at Cove Rock	*Dugmore*	87
"Should it be according to Thy mind"	*Selwyn*	134
Sight from the Shore	*Dugmore*	82
Sonnets of the Cape	*Longmore*	123
South Africa Rediviva	*Wilmot*	113
Southern Cross	*Cruikshanks*	176
Storm in Tugela Valley	*Moodie*	190
Sunny Hills of Africa	*Hartwell*	175
Sunrise at Cove Rock	*Dugmore*	79
Sunset (An Ocean)	,,	81
"Teuton" (The Gallant)	*Hartwell*	174
Thunderstorm	*Dugmore*	82
Volunteers of England	,,	53
Welcome	*Bidwell*	256
Wilderness (S. African)	*Dugmore*	77
Zulu War	*Selwyn*	137

POEMS.

THE EMIGRANTS.

. . . . . . The sire has told
  The heart-struck group of dark disaster nigh:
Their old paternal home must now be sold,
    And that last relic of ancestry
Resigned to strangers. Long and strenuously
  He strove to stem the flood's o'erwhelming mass;
But still some fresh unseen calamity
    Burst like a foaming billow—till, alas!
    No hope remains that this their sorest grief may pass.

" Yet be not thus dismayed. Our altered lot
    He that ordains will brace us to endure.
This changeful world affords no sheltered spot,
    Where man may count his frail possessions sure:
Our better birthright, noble, precious, pure,
    May well console for earthly treasures marred,—
Treasures, alas! how vain and insecure,
    Where none from rust and robbery can guard:
    The wise man looks to heaven alone for his reward."

The Christian father thus.   But whither now
   Shall the bewildered band their course direct?
What home shall shield that matron's honoured brow,
   And those dear pensive maids from wrong protect?
Or cheer them 'mid the world's unkind neglect?
   That world to the unfortunate so cold,
While lavish of its smiles and fair respect
   Unto the proud, the prosperous, the bold;
     Still shunning want and woe; still courting pomp and gold.

Shall they adopt the poor retainer's trade,
   And sue for pity from the great and proud?
No! never shall ungenerous souls upbraid
   Their conduct in adversity—which bowed
But not debased them.   Or, amidst the crowd,
   In noisome towns shall they themselves immure,
Their wounds, their woes, their weary days to shroud
   In some mean melancholy nook obscure?
     No! worthier tasks await, and brighter scenes allure.

A land of climate fair and fertile soil,
   Teeming with milk and wine and waving corn,
Invites from far the venturous Briton's toil:
   And thousands, long by fruitless cares foresworn,
And now across the wide Atlantic borne,
   To seek new homes on Afric's southern strand:
Better to launch with them than sink forlorn
   To vile dependence in our native land;
     Better to fall in God's than man's unfeeling hand!

With hearts resigned they tranquilly prepare
   To share the fortunes of that exile train.

And soon with many a follower, forth they fare—
   High hope and courage in their hearts again :
And now, afloat upon the dark-blue main,
   They gaze upon the fast-receding shore
With tearful eyes—while thus the ballad strain,
   Half heard amidst the ocean's weltering roar,
   Bids farewell to the scenes they ne'er shall visit more :—

   " Our native land—our native vale—
      A long and last adieu !
   Farewell to bonny Teviot-dale,
      And Cheviot mountains blue !

   " Farewell, ye hills of glorious deeds,
      And streams renowned in song ;
   Farewell, ye blithesome braes and meads
      Our hearts have loved so long.

   " Farewell, ye broomy elfin knowes,
      Where thyme and harebells grow !
   Farewell, ye hoary haunted howes,
      O'erhung with birk and sloe.

   " The battle-mound, the Border-tower,
      That Scotia's annals tell ;
   The martyr's grave, the lover's bower—
      To each—to all—farewell !

   " Home of our hearts ! our father's home !
      Land of the brave and free !
   The sale is flapping on the foam
      That bears us far from thee !

" We seek a wild and distant shore
    Beyond the Atlantic main;
We leave thee to return no more,
    Nor view thy cliffs again:

" But may dishonour blight our fame,
    And quench our household fires,
When we, or ours, forget thy name,
    Green Island of our Sires.

" Our native land—our native vale—
    A long, a last adieu!
Farewell to bonny Teviot-dale,
    And Scotland's mountains blue."

Thomas Pringle.

HUNTSCHAW, *Sept.* 20, 1819.

THE BECHUANA BOY.

I SAT at noontide in my tent,
    And looked across the desert dun,
Beneath the cloudless firmament
    Far gleaming in the sun,
When from the bosom of the waste
A swarthy stripling came in haste,
With foot unshod and naked limb;
·And a tame springbok followed him.

With open aspect, frank yet bland,
    And with a modest mien he stood,

Caressing with a gentle hand
   That beast of gentle brood;
Then, meekly gazing in my face,
Said in the language of his race,
With smiling look yet pensive tone,
"Stranger—I'm in the world alone!"

"Poor boy," I said, "thy native home
   Lies far beyond the Stormberg blue:
Why hast thou left it, boy! to roam
   This desolate Karroo?"
His face grew sadder while I spoke;
The smile forsook it; and he broke
Short silence with a sob-like sigh,
And told his hapless history.

"I have no home!" replied the boy;
   "The Bergenaars—by night they came,
And raised their wolfish howl of joy,
   While o'er our huts the flame
Resistless rushed; and aye their yell
Pealed louder as our warriors fell
In helpless heaps beneath their shot:
—One living man they left us not!

"The slaughter o'er, they gave the slain
   To feast the foul-beaked birds of prey,
And with our herds across the plain
   They hurried us away—
The widowed mothers and their brood.
Oft, in despair, for drink or food
We vainly cried; they heeded not,
But with sharp lash the captive smote.

"Three days we tracked that dreary wild,
   Where thirst and anguish pressed us sore;
And many a mother and her child
   Lay down to rise no more.
Behind us, on the desert brown,
We saw the vultures swooping down;
And heard, as the grim night was falling,
The wolf to his gorged comrade calling.

" At length was heard a river sounding
   'Midst that dry and dismal land,
And, like a troop of wild deer bounding,
   We hurried to its strand—
Among the maddened cattle rushing,
The crowd behind still forward pushing,
Till in the flood our limbs were drenched
And the fierce rage of thirst was quenched.

" Hoarse roaring, dark, the broad Gareep
   In turbid streams was sweeping fast,
Huge sea-cows in its eddies deep
   Loud snorting as we passed;
But that relentless robber clan
Right through those waters wild and wan
Drove on like sheep our wearied band:
—Some never reached the farther strand.

" All shivering from the foaming flood,
   We stood upon the strangers' ground,
When, with proud looks and gestures rude,
   The white men gathered round:
And there, like cattle from the fold,
By Christians we were bought and sold,

'Midst laughter loud and looks of scorn—
And roughly from each other torn.

" My mother's scream, so long and shrill,
   My little sister's wailing cry
(In dreams I often hear them still !),
   Rose wildly to the sky.
A tiger's heart came to me then,
And fiercely on those ruthless men
I sprang—alas ! dashed on the sand
Bleeding, they bound me foot and hand.

" Away, away on prancing steeds
   The stout man-stealers blithely go,
Through long low valleys fringed with reeds,
   O'er mountains capped with snow
Each with his captive, far and fast ;
Until yon rock-bound ridge we passed,
And distant strips of cultured soil
Bespoke the land of tears and toil.

" And tears and toil have been my lot
   Since I the white-man's thrall became,
And sorer griefs I wish forgot—
   Harsh blows, and scorn, and shame !
Oh, Englishman ! thou ne'er canst know
The injured bondman's bitter woe,
When round his breast, like scorpions, cling
Black thoughts that madden while they sting !

" Yet this hard fate I might have borne,
   And taught in time my soul to bend,
Had my sad yearning heart forlorn
   But found a single friend :

My race extinct or far removed,
The Boer's rough brood I could have loved;
But each to whom my bosom turned
Even like a hound the black boy spurned.

"While, friendless, thus, my master's flocks
   I tended on the upland waste,
It chanced this fawn leapt from the rocks,
   By wolfish wild-dogs chased:
I rescued it, though wounded sore
And dabbled in its mother's gore;
And nursed it in a cavern wild,
Until it loved me like a child.

"Gently I nursed it; for I thought
   (Its hapless fate so like to mine)
By good Utíko * it was brought
   To bid me not repine,—
Since in this world of wrong and ill
One creature lived that loved me still,
Although its dark and dazzling eye
Beamed not with human sympathy.

"Thus lived I, a lone orphan lad,
   My task the proud Boer's flocks to tend;
And this poor fawn was all I had
   To love or call my friend;
When suddenly, with haughty look
And taunting words, that tyrant took
My playmate for his pampered boy,
Who envied me my only joy.

---

    * Utíko,—Hottentot name for God.

" High swelled my heart!—But when the star
   Of midnight gleamed, I softly led
My bounding favourite forth, and far
   Into the desert fled.
And here, from human kind exiled,
Three moons on roots and berries wild
I've fared; and braved the beasts of prey,
To 'scape from spoilers worse than they.

" But yester morn a Bushman brought
   The tidings that thy tents were near;
And now with hasty foot I've sought
   Thy presence, void of fear;
Because they say, O English chief,
Thou scornest not the captive's grief:
Then let me serve thee, as thine own—
For I am in the world alone!"

Such was Marossi's touching tale.
   Our breasts they were not made of stone:
His words, his winning looks prevail—
   We took him for "our own."
And one, with woman's gentle art,
Unlocked the fountains of his heart;
And love gushed forth—till he became
Her child in everything but name.

Thomas Pringle.

AFAR IN THE DESERT.

Afar in the desert I love to ride,
With the silent Bush-boy alone by my side:
When the sorrows of life the soul o'ercast,
And, sick of the Present, I cling to the past;
When the eye is suffused with regretful tears,
From the fond recollections of former years;
And shadows of things that have long since fled
Flit over the brain, like the ghosts of the dead:
Bright visions of glory—that vanished too soon;
Day dreams—that departed ere manhood's noon;
Attachments—by fate or by falsehood reft;
Companions of early days—lost or left;
And my native Land—whose magical name
Thrills to the heart like electric flame;
The home of my childhood; the haunts of my prime;
All the passions and scenes of that rapturous time
When the feelings were young and the world was new,
Like the fresh flowers of Eden unfolding to view;
All—all now forsaken—forgotten—foregone!
And I—a lone exile remembered by none—
My high aims abandoned,—my good acts undone,—
Aweary of all that is under the sun,—
With that sadness of heart which no stranger may scan,
I fly to the desert, afar from man!

Afar in the desert I love to ride,
With the silent Bush-boy alone by my side:
When the wild turmoil of this wearisome life,
With its scenes of oppression, corruption, and strife—

The proud man's frown, and the base man's fear,—
The scorner's laugh, and the sufferer's tear,—
And malice, and meanness, and falsehood, and folly,
Dispose me to musing and dark melancholy;
When my bosom is full, and my thoughts are high,
And my soul is sick with the bondsman's sigh—
Oh! then there is freedom, and joy, and pride,
Afar in the desert alone to ride!
There is rapture to vault on the champing steed,
And to bound away with the eagle's speed,
With the death-fraught firelock in my hand—
The only law in the Desert Land!

Afar in the desert I love to ride,
With the silent Bush-boy alone by my side:
Away, away, from the dwellings of men,
By the wild deer's haunt, by the buffalo's glen;
By valleys remote where the oribi plays,
Where the gnu, the gazelle, and the hartebeest graze,
And the kùdù and eland unhunted recline
By the skirts of grey forests o'erhung with wild vine;
Where the elephant browses at peace in his wood,
And the river-horse gambols unscared in the flood,
And the mighty rhinoceros wallows at will
In the fen where the wild ass is drinking his fill.

Afar in the desert I love to ride,
With the silent Bush-boy alone by my side:
O'er the brown Karroo, where the bleating cry
Of the springbok's fawn sounds plaintively;
And the timorous quagga's shrill whistling neigh
Is heard by the fountain at twilight grey;

Where the zebra wantonly tosses his mane,
With wild hoof scouring the desolate plain;
And the fleet-footed ostrich over the waste
Speeds like a horseman who travels in haste,
Hieing away to the home of her rest,
Where she and her mate have scooped their nest,
Far hid from the pitiless plunderer's view
In the pathless depths of the parched Karroo.

Afar in the desert I love to ride,
With the silent Bush-boy alone by my side:
Away, away, in the wilderness vast,
Where the white man's foot hath never passed,
And the quivered Coránna or Bechuán
Hath rarely crossed with his roving clan:
A region of emptiness, howling and drear,
Which man hath abandoned from famine and fear;
Which the snake and the lizard inhabit alone,
With the twilight bat from the yawning stone;
Where grass, nor herb, nor shrub takes root,
Save poisonous thorns that pierce the foot;
And the bitter-melon, for food and drink,
Is the pilgrim's fare by the salt lake's brink:
A region of drought, where no river glides,
Nor rippling brook with osiered sides;
Where sedgy pool, nor bubbling fount,
Nor tree, nor cloud, nor misty mount,
Appears, to refresh the aching eye:
But the barren earth, and the burning sky,
And the blank horizon, round and round,
Spread—void of living sight and sound,
And here, while the night-winds round me sigh,
And the stars burn bright in the midnight sky,

As I sit apart by the desert stone,
Like Elijah at Horeb's cave alone,
" A still small voice" comes through the wild
(Like a father consoling his fretful child),
Which banishes bitterness, wrath, and fear,—
Saying—MAN IS DISTANT, BUT GOD IS NEAR!

Thomas Pringle.

EVENING RAMBLES.

THE sultry summer-noon is past;
And mellow evening comes at last,
With a low and languid breeze
Fanning the mimosa trees,
That cluster o'er the yellow vale,
And oft perfume the panting gale
With fragrance faint: it seems to tell
Of primrose-tufts in Scottish dell,
Peeping forth in tender spring
When the blithe lark begins to sing.

But soon, amidst our Libyan vale,
Such soothing recollections fail;
Soon we raise the eye to range
O'er prospects wild, grotesque, and strange:
Sterile mountains, rough and steep,
That bound abrupt the valley deep,
Heaving to the clear blue sky
Their ribs of granite, bare and dry,

And ridges by the torrents worn,
Thinly streaked with scraggy thorn,
Which fringes nature's savage dress,
Yet scarce relieves her nakedness.

But where the vale winds deep below
The landscape hath a warmer glow:
There the spekboom spreads its bowers
Of light green leaves and lilac flowers;
And the aloe rears her crimson crest,
Like stately queen for gala drest;
And the bright-blossomed bean-tree shakes
Its coral tufts above the brakes,
Brilliant as the glancing plumes
Of sugar birds among its blooms,
With the deep green verdure bending
In the stream of light descending.

And now along the grassy meads,
Where the skipping reebok feeds,
Let me through the mazes rove
Of the light acacia grove;
Now while yet the honey-bee
Hums around the blossomed tree;
And the turtles softly chide,
Wooingly, on every side;
And the clucking pheasant calls
To his mate at intervals;
And the duiker at my tread
Sudden lifts his startled head,
Then dives affrighted in the brake,
Like wild duck in the reedy lake.

My wonted seat receives me now—
This cliff with myrtle-tufted brow,
Towering high o'er grove and stream,
As if to greet the parting gleam.
With shattered rocks besprinkled o'er,
Behind ascends the mountain hoar,
Whose crest o'erhangs the Bushman's cave
(His fortress once and now his grave),
Where the grim satyr-faced baboon
Sits gibbering on the rising moon,
Or chides with hoarse and angry cry
The herdsman as he wanders by.

Spread out below in sun and shade,
The shaggy Glen lies full displayed—
Its sheltered nooks, its sylvan bowers,
Its meadows flushed with purple flowers;
And through it like a dragon spread,
I trace the river's tortuous bed.
Lo! there the Chaldee-willow weeps
Drooping o'er the headlong steeps,
Where the torrent in his wrath
Hath rifted him a rugged path,
Like fissure cleft by earthquake's shock,
Through mead and jungle, mound and rock.
But the swoln water's wasteful sway,
Like tyrant's rage, hath passed away,
And left the ravage of its course
Memorial of its frantic force.
—Now o'er its shrunk and slimy bed
Rank weeds and withered wrack are spread,
With the faint rill just oozing through,
And vanishing again from view;

Save where the guana's glassy pool
Holds to some cliff its mirror cool,
Girt by the palmite's leafy screen,
Or graceful rock-ash, tall and green,
Whose slender sprays above the flood
Suspend the loxia's callow brood
In cradle-nests, with porch below,
Secure from winged or creeping foe—
Weasel or hawk or writhing snake;
Light swinging, as the breezes wake,
Like the ripe fruit we love to see
Upon the rich pomegranate tree.

But lo! the sun's descending car
Sinks o'er Mount Dunion's peaks afar;
And now along the dusky vale
The homeward herds and flocks I hail,
Returning from their pastures dry
Amid the stony uplands high.
First, the brown Herder with his flock
Comes winding round my hermit-rock:
His mien and gait and gesture tell,
No shepherd he from Scottish fell;
For crook the guardian gun he bears,
For plaid the sheepskin mantle wears;
Sauntering languidly along;
Nor flute has he, nor merry song,
Nor book, nor tale, nor rustic lay,
To cheer him through his listless day.
His look is dull, his soul is dark;
He feels not hope's electric spark;
But, born the white man's servile thrall,
Knows that he cannot lower fall.

Next the stout Neat-herd passes by,
With bolder step and blither eye;
Humming low his tuneless song,
Or whistling to the hornèd throng.
From the destroying foeman fled,—
He serves the Colonist for bread:
Yet this poor heathen Bechuan
Bears on his brow the port of man;
A naked homeless exile he—
But not debased by slavery.

Now, wizard-like, slow Twilight sails
With soundless wing adown the vales,
Waving with his shadowy rod
The owl and bat to come abroad,
With things that hate the garish sun,
To frolic now when day is done.
Now along the meadows damp
The enamoured firefly lights his lamp.
Link-boy he of woodland green
To light fair Avon's Elfin Queen;
Here, I ween, more wont to shine
To light the thievish porcupine,
Plundering my melon-bed,—
Or villain lynx, whose stealthy tread
Rouses not the wakeful hound
As he creeps the folds around.

But lo! the night-bird's boding scream
Breaks abrupt my twilight dream;
And warns me it is time to haste
My homeward walk across the waste,

Lest my rash step provoke the wrath
Of adder coiled upon the path,
Or tempt the lion from the wood,
That soon will prowl athirst for blood,
—Thus, murmuring my thoughtful strain,
I seek our wattled cot again.

Thomas Pringle.

GLEN LYNDEN, 1822.

THE LION HUNT.

MOUNT—mount for the hunting with musket and spear!
Call our friends to the field—for the lion is near!
Call Arend and Ekhard and Groepe to the spoor;
Call Muller and Coetzer and Lucas Van Vuur.

Ride up Eildon-Cleugh, and blow loudly the bugle:
Call Slinger and Allie and Dikkop and Dugal;
And George with the Elephant-gun on his shoulder—
In a perilous pinch none is better or bolder.

In the gorge of the glen lie the bones of my steed,
And the hoof of a heifer of fatherland's breed:
But mount, my brave boys, if our rifles prove true,
We'll soon make the spoiler his ravages rue.

Ho! the Hottentot lads have discovered the track—
To his den in the desert we'll follow him back;
But tighten your girths, and look well to your flints,
For heavy and fresh are the villain's foot-prints.

THE LION HUNT.

Through the rough rocky kloof into grey Huntly-Glen,
Past the wild-olive clump where the wolf has his den,
By the black eagle's rock at the foot of the fell,
We have tracked him at last to the buffalo's well.

Now mark yonder brake where the bloodhounds are howling;
And hark that hoarse sound—like the deep thunder growling;
'Tis his lair—'tis his voice!—from your saddles alight;
He's at bay in the brushwood preparing for fight.

Leave the horses behind—and be still every man;
Let the Mullers and Rennies advance in the van:
Keep fast in your ranks;—by the yell of yon hound,
The savage, I guess, will be out—with a bound.

He comes! the tall jungle before him loud crashing,
His mane bristled fiercely, his fiery eyes flashing;
With a roar of disdain, he leaps forth in his wrath,
To challenge the foe that dare 'leaguer his path.

He couches,—ay, now we'll see mischief, I dread:
Quick—level your rifles—and aim at his head:
Thrust forward the spears, and unsheath every knife—
St. George! he's upon us!—now, fire, lads, for life!

He's wounded—but yet he'll draw blood ere he falls—
Ha! under his paw see Bezudenhout sprawls—
Now Diederik! Christian! right in the brain
Plant each man his bullet—Hurra! he is slain!

Bezudenhout—up, man!—'tis only a scratch—
(You were always a scamp and have met with your match!)
What a glorious lion!—what sinews—what claws—
And seven feet ten from the rump to the jaws!

His hide, with the paws and the bones of his skull,
With the spoils of the leopard and buffalo bull,
We'll send to Sir Walter—now, boys, let us dine,
And talk of our deeds o'er a flask of old wine.

Thomas Pringle.

THE LION AND THE GIRAFFE.

WOULDST thou view the lion's den?
Search afar from haunts of men—
Where the reed-encircled rill
Oozes from the rocky hill,
By its verdure far descried
'Mid the desert brown and wide.

Close beside the sedgy brim
Couchant lurks the lion grim;
Watching till the close of day
Brings the death-devoted prey.
Heedless at the ambushed brink
The tall giraffe stoops down to drink.

Upon him straight the savage springs
With cruel joy. The desert rings
With clanging sound of desperate strife—
The prey is strong and he strives for life.

THE LION AND THE GIRAFFE.

Plunging oft with frantic bound,
To shake the tyrant to the ground,
He shrieks, he rushes through the waste,
With glaring eye and headlong haste:
In vain!—the spoiler on his prize
Rides proudly—tearing as he flies.

For life—the victim's utmost speed
Is mustered in this hour of need:
For life—for life—his giant might
He strains, and pours his soul in flight:
And mad with terror, thirst and pain,
Spurns with wild hoof the thundering plain.

'Tis vain; the thirsty sands are drinking
His streaming blood—his strength is sinking;
The victor's fangs are in his veins—
His flanks are streaked with sanguine stains—
His panting breast in foam and gore
Is bathed—he reels—his race is o'er:
He falls—and, with convulsive throe,
Resigns his throat to the ravening foe!
—And lo! ere quivering life has fled,
The vultures, wheeling overhead,
Swoop down, to watch, in gaunt array,
Till the gorged tyrant quits his prey.

Thomas Pringle.

THE DESOLATE VALLEY.

Far up among the forest-belted mountains,
Where Winterberg, stern giant old and grey,
Looks down the subject dells, whose gleaming fountains
To wizard Kat their virgin tribute pay,
A valley opens to the noontide ray,
With green savannahs shelving to the brim
Of the swift river, sweeping on its way
To where Umtóka* tries to meet with him,
Like a blue serpent gliding through the acacias dim.

Round this secluded region circling rise
Are billowy wastes of mountains, wild and wide;
Upon whose grassy slopes the pilgrim spies
The gnu and quagga, by the greenwood side,
Tossing their shaggy manes in tameless pride;
Or troop of elands near some sedgy fount;
Or Kùdù fawns, that from the thicket glide.
To seek their dam upon the misty mount,
With harts, gazelles, and roes, more than the eye can count.

And as we journeyed up the pathless glen,
Flanked by romantic hills on either hand,
The boschbok oft would bound away—and then
Beside the willows, backward gazing, stand.
And where old forests darken all the land
From rocky Kalberg to the river's brink,

---

* A branch of the Kat River.

THE DESOLATE VALLEY.

 The buffalo would start upon the strand,
 Where, 'mid palmetto flags, he stooped to drink,
And, crashing through the brakes, to the deep jungle
  shrink.

 Then, couched at night in hunter's wattled sheiling,
 How wildly beautiful it was to hear
 The elephant his shrill *réveillé* pealing,
 Like some far signal-trumpet on the ear!
 While the broad midnight moon was shining clear,
 How fearful to look forth upon the woods,
 And see those stately forest-kings appear,
 Emerging from their shadowy solitudes—
As if that trump had woke Earth's old gigantic broods!

 Such the majestic, melancholy scene
 Which 'midst that mountain-wilderness we found;
 With scarce a trace to tell where man had been,
 Save the old Caffer cabins crumbling round.
 Yet this lone glen (Sicāna's ancient ground)
 To nature's savage tribes abandoned long,
 Had heard, erewhile, the Gospel's joyful sound,
 And low of herds mixed with the Sabbath song.
But all is silent now. The oppressor's hand was strong.

 Now the blithe loxia hangs her pensile nest
 From the wild-olive, bending o'er the rock,
 Beneath whose shadow, in grave mantle drest,
 The Christian pastor taught his swarthy flock.
 A roofless ruin, scathed by flame and smoke,
 Tells where a decent mission-chapel stood;
 While the baboon with jabbering cry doth mock
 The pilgrim, pausing in his pensive mood
To ask—"Why is it thus? Shall EVIL baffle GOOD?"

Yes—for a season Satan may prevail,
And hold, as if secure, his dark domain;
The prayers of righteous men may seem to fail,
And Heaven's glad tidings be proclaimed in vain.
But wait in faith: ere long shall spring again
The seed that seemed to perish in the ground;
And fertilised by Zion's latter rain,
The long-parched land shall laugh, with harvests crowned,
And through those silent wastes Jehovah's praise resound.

Look round that vale: behold the unburied bones
Of Ghona's children withering in the blast:
The sobbing wind, that through the forest moans,
Whispers—"The spirit hath for ever passed!"
Thus, in the vale of desolation vast,
In moral death dark Afric's myriads lie;
But the appointed day shall dawn at last,
When breathed on by a spirit from on high,
The dry bones shall awake, and shout—"Our God is nigh!"

Thomas Pringle.

THE CORANNA.

FAST by his wild resounding river
The listless Córan lingers ever;
Still drives his heifers forth to feed,
Soothed by the gorrah's humming reed;*

---

* A musical instrument peculiar to the Hottentot tribes.

A rover still unchecked will range,
As humour calls, or seasons change;
His tent of mats and leathern gear
All packed upon the patient steer.
'Mid all his wanderings hating toil,
He never tills the stubborn soil;
But on the milky dams relies,
And what spontaneous earth supplies.
Should some long parching droughts prevail,
And milk and bulbs and locusts fail,
He lays him down to sleep away
In languid trance the weary day;
Oft as he feels gaunt hunger's stound,*
Still tightening famine's girdle round;
Lulled by the sound of the Gareep,
Beneath the willows murmuring deep:
Till thunder-clouds surcharged with rain,
Pour verdure o'er the panting plain;
And call the famished dreamer from his trance,
To feast on milk and game, and wake the moonlight
    dance.

Thomas Pringle.

SONG OF THE WILD BUSHMAN.

L<small>ET</small> the proud white man boast his flocks,
    And fields of foodful grain;
My home is 'mid the mountain rocks,
    The desert my domain.

---

* Stound—a sharp pang, a shooting pain.

I plant no herbs nor pleasant fruits,
    I toil not for my cheer;
The desert yields me juicy roots,
    And herds of bounding deer.

The countless springboks are my flock,
    Spread o'er the unbounded plain;
The buffalo bendeth to my yoke,
    The wild horse to my rein;*
My yoke is the quivering assegai,
    My rein the tough bow-string;
My bridle curb a slender barb—
    Yet it quells the forest king.
The crested adder honoureth me,
    And yields at my command
His poison bag, like the honey-bee,
    When I seize him on the sand.
Yea, even the wasting locust-swarm,
    Which mighty nations dread,
To me nor terror brings, nor harm—
    For I make of them my bread.†

Thus I am lord of the Desert Land,
    And I will not leave my bounds,
To crouch beneath the Christian's hand,
    And kennel with his hounds:
To be a hound, and watch the flocks,
    For the cruel white man's gain—

---

* The zebra is commonly termed *Wilde-Paard*, or wild horse, by the Dutch African colonists.

† The Bushmen consider the locusts a great luxury, consuming great quantities fresh, and drying abundance for future emergencies.

No! the brown Serpent of the Rocks
   His den doth yet retain;
And none who there his stings provokes
   Shall find his poison vain!

Thomas Pringle.

THE CAPTIVE OF CAMALÚ.

O CAMALÚ—green Camalú!
   'Twas there I fed my father's flock,
Beside the mount where cedars threw
   At dawn their shadows from the rock;
There tended I my father's flock
   Along the grassy margined rills,
Or chased the bounding bontébok
   With hound and spear among the hills.

Green Camalú! methinks I view
   The lilies in thy meadows growing;
I see thy waters bright and blue
   Beneath the pale-leaved willows flowing;
I hear along the valleys lowing,
   The heifers wending to the fold,
And jocund herd-boys loudly blowing
   The horn—to mimic hunters bold.

Methinks I see the umkóba tree *
   That shades the village-chieftain's cot;
The evening smoke curls lovingly
   Above that calm and pleasant spot.

---

* Caffer name for the yellow-wood tree.

My father?—Ha!—I had forgot—
   The old man rests in slumber deep:
My mother?—Ay! she answers not—
   Her heart is hushed in dreamless sleep.

My brothers too—green Camalú,
   Repose they by thy quiet tide?
Ay! there they sleep—where white men slew
   And left them—lying side by side.
No pity had those men of pride,
   They fired the huts above the dying!—
While bones bestrew that valley wide—
   I wish that mine were with them lying!

I envy you by Camalú,
   Ye wild harts on the woody hills;
Though tigers there their prey pursue,
   And vultures slake in blood their bills.
The heart may strive in Nature's ills,
   To Nature's common doom resigned:
Death the frail body only kills—
   But thraldom brutifies the mind.

Oh, wretched fate!—heart desolate,
   A captive in the spoiler's hand,
To serve the tyrant, whom I hate—
   To crouch beneath his proud command—
Upon my flesh to bear his brand—
   His blows, his bitter scorn to bide!—
Would God I in my native land
   Had with my slaughtered brothers died!

THE CAPTIVE OF CAMALÚ.

Ye mountains blue of Camalú,
   Where once I fed my father's flock,
Though desolation dwells with you,
   And Amakósa's heart is broke,
Yet, spite of chains these limbs that mock,
   My homeless heart to you doth fly,—
As flies the wild dove to the rock,
   To hide its wounded breast—and die!

Yet, ere my spirit wings its flight
   Unto 'Death's silent shadowy clime,
Utſko! Lord of life and light,
   Who, high above the clouds of Time,
Calm sittest, where yon hosts sublime
   Of stars wheel round thy bright abode,
Oh, let my cry unto thee climb,
   Of every race the Father-God!

I ask not judgments from thy hand—
   Destroying hail or parching drought,
Or locust swarms to waste the land,
   Or pestilence, by Famine brought;
I say the prayer Jankanna* taught,
   Who wept for Amakósa's wrongs—
"Thy kingdom come—Thy will be wrought—
   For unto Thee all power belongs."

Thy kingdom come! Let Light and Grace
   Throughout all lands in triumph go;
Till pride and strife to love give place,
   And blood and tears forget to flow;

---

* Name given to the missionary, Van der Kemp, by the Caffers.

Till Europe mourn for Afric's woe,
  And o'er the deep her arms extend
To lift her where she lieth low,
  And prove indeed her Christian Friend!

Thomas Pringle.

THE BROWN HUNTER'S SONG.

UNDER the Didima * lies a green dell,
Where fresh from the forest the blue waters swell;
And fast by that brook stands a yellow-wood tree
Which shelters the spot which is dearest to me.

Down by the streamlet my heifers are grazing;
In the pool of the guanas the herd-boy is gazing;
Under the shade my amana is singing—
The shade of the tree where her cradle is swinging.

When I come from the upland as daylight is fading,
Though spent with the chase, and the game for my lading,
My nerves are new-strung and my fond heart is swelling
As I gaze from the cliff on our wood-circled dwelling.

Down the steep mountain and through the brown forest,
I haste like a hart when his thirst is the sorest;
I bound o'er the swift brook that skirts the savannah,
And clasp my first-born in the arms of Amana.

Thomas Pringle.

---

  * Mountain between the sources of the Kat and Koonap rivers.

THE BUSHMAN.

THE Bushman sleeps within his black-browed den,
In the lone wilderness. Around him lie
His wife and little ones unfearingly—
For they are far away from "Christian men."
No herds, loud lowing, call him down the glen:
He fears no foe but famine; and may try
To wear away the hot noon slumberingly;
Then rise to search for roots—and dance again.
But he shall dance no more! His secret lair,
Surrounded, echoes to the thundering gun,
And the wild shriek of anguish and despair!
He dies—yet, ere life's ebbing sands are run,
Leaves to his sons a curse, should they be friends
With the proud "Christian men,"—for they are fiends!

Thomas Pringle.

THE CAPE OF STORMS.

O CAPE of Storms! although thy front be dark,
And bleak thy naked cliffs and cheerless vales,
And perilous thy fierce and faithless gales
To staunchest mariner and stoutest bark;
And though along thy coasts with grief I mark
The servile and the slave, and him who wails
An exile's lot—and blush to hear thy tales
Of sin and sorrow and oppression stark:—
Yet, spite of physical and moral ill,
And after all I've seen and suffered here,

There are strong links that bind me to thee still,
And render even thy rocks and deserts dear;
Here dwell kind hearts which time nor place can chill—
Loved kindred and congenial friends sincere.

Thomas Pringle, 1825.

THE HOTTENTOT.

MILD, melancholy, and sedate, he stands,
Tending another's flock upon the fields,
His fathers' once, where now the white man builds
His home, and issues forth his proud commands.
His dark eye flashes not; his listless hands
Lean on the shepherd's staff; no more he wields
The Libyan bow—but to th' oppressor yields
Submissively his freedom and his lands.
Has he no courage? Once he had—but, lo!
Harsh servitude hath worn him to the bone.
No enterprise? Alas! the brand, the blow,
Hath humbled him to dust—even *hope* is gone!
"He's a base-hearted hound—not worth his food"—
His master cries; "he has no *gratitude!*"

Thomas Pringle.

THE CAFFER.

LO! where he crouches by the Kloof's dark side,
Eyeing the farmer's lowing herds, afar;
Impatient watching till the evening star
Leads forth the twilight dim, that he may glide

Like panther to the prey.   With freeborn pride
He scorns the herdsman, nor regards the scar
Of recent wound—but burnishes for war
His assegai and targe of buffalo hide.
He is a robber?   True; it is a strife
Between the black skinned bandit and the white.
A savage?—Yes; though loth to aim at life,
Evil for evil fierce he doth requite.
A heathen?—Teach him, then, thy better creed,
Christian! if thou deserv'st that name indeed.

Thomas Pringle.

THE GHONA WIDOW'S LULLABY.

The storm hath ceased: yet still I hear
   The distant thunder sounding,
And from the mountains, far and near,
   The headlong torrents bounding.
The jackal shrieks upon the rocks,
   The tiger wolf is howling,
The panther round the folded flocks
   With stifled *gurr* is prowling.
But lay thee down in peace, my child,
God watcheth o'er us 'midst the wild.

I fear the Bushman is abroad—
   He loves the midnight thunder;
The sheeted lightning shows the road
   That leads his feet to plunder:
I'd rather meet the hooded snake
   Than hear his rattling quiver,

When, like an adder, through the brake,
   He glides along the river.
But, darling, hush thy heart to sleep—
The Lord our Shepherd watch doth keep.

The Kosa from Luhéri high
   Looks down upon our dwelling,
And shakes the vengeful assegai,—
   Unto his clansmen telling
How he, for *us*, by grievous wrong,
   Hath lost these fertile valleys,
And boasts that now his hand is strong
   To pay the debt of malice.
But sleep, my child; a mightier Arm
Shall shield thee (helpless one!) from harm.

The moon is up; a fleecy cloud
   O'er heaven's blue deep is sailing;
The stream, that lately raved so loud,
   Makes now a gentle wailing.
From yonder crags, lit by the moon,
   I hear a wild voice crying:
—'Tis but the harmless bear-baboon,
   Unto his mates replying.
Hush—hush thy dreams, my moaning dove,
And slumber in the arms of love!

The wolf, scared by the watch-dog's bay,
   Is to the woods returning:
By his rock fortress, far away,
   The Bushman's fire is burning.

THE GHONA WIDOW'S LULLABY.

And hark! Sicána's midnight hymn,
    Along the valley swelling,
Calls us to stretch the wearied limb,
    While kinsmen guard our dwelling:
Though vainly watchmen wake from sleep,
" Unless the Lord the city keep."

At dawn we'll seek, with songs of praise,
    Our food on the savannah,
As Israel sought, in ancient days,
    The heaven-descending manna;
With gladness from the fertile land
    The veld-kost we will gather,
A harvest planted by the hand
    Of the Almighty Father—
From thraldom who redeems our race,
To plant them in their ancient place.

Then let us calmly rest, my child,
    Jehovah's arm is round us,
The God, the Father reconciled,
    In heathen gloom who found us;
Who to this heart, by sorrow broke,
    His wondrous WORD revealing,
Led me, a lost sheep, to the flock,
    And to the Fount of Healing.
Oh, may the Saviour-Shepherd lead
My darling where His lambs do feed!

                  Thomas Pringle.

THE KOSA.

The free-born Kosa still doth hold
The fields his fathers held of old;
With club and spear in jocund ranks,
Still hunts the elk by Chumi's banks:
By Keisis meads his herds are lowing;
On Debè's slopes his gardens glowing,
Where laughing maids at sunset roam,
To bear the juicy melons home:
And striplings from Kalunna's wood
Bring wild grapes and the pigeon's brood,
With fragrant hoards of honey-bee
Rifled from the hollow tree:
And herdsmen shout from rock to rock:
And through the glen the hamlets smoke;
And children gambol round the kraal,*
To greet their sires at evening-fall:
And matrons sweep the cabin floor,
And spread the mat beside the door,
And with dry faggots wake the flame
To dress the wearied huntsman's game.

Bright gleams the fire: its ruddy blaze
On many a dusky visage plays.
On forkèd twigs the game is drest;
The neighbours share the simple feast:
The honey-mead, the millet-ale,
Flow round—and flow the jest and tale;

---

* Kraal or cattle-fold; also a native village or encampment.

Wild legends of the ancient day,
Of hunting feat, of warlike fray;
And now come smiles, and now come sighs,
As mirth and grief alternate rise.
Or should a sterner strain awake,
Like sudden flame in summer-brake,
Bursts fiercely forth in battle song
The tale of Amakósa's wrong;
Throbs every warrior bosom high,
With lightning flashes every eye,
And, in wild cadence, rings the sound
Of barbèd javelins clashing round.

But, lo! like a broad shield on high,
The moon gleams in the midnight sky.
'Tis time to part; the watch-dog's bay
Beside the folds has died away.
'Tis time to rest; the mat is spread,
The hardy hunter's simple bed;
His wife her dreaming infant hushes,
On the low cabin's couch of rushes:
Softly he draws its door of hide,
And, stretched by his Gulúwi's side,
Sleeps soundly till the peep of dawn
Wakes on the hill the dappled fawn;
Then forth again he gaily bounds,
With club and spear and questing hounds.

Thomas Pringle.

MAKANNA'S GATHERING.

Wake! Amakósa, wake!
    And arm yourselves for war,
As coming winds the forest shake,
    I hear a sound from far:
It is not thunder in the sky,
    Nor lion's roar upon the hill,
But the voice of Him who sits on high,
    And bids me speak His will!

He bids me call you forth,
    Bold sons of Káhabee,
To sweep the white men from the earth,
    And drive them to the sea:
The sea which heaved them up at first,
    For Amakósa's curse and bane,
Howls for the progeny she nurst,
    To swallow them again.

Hark! 'tis Uhlanga's voice
    From Debé's mountain caves!
He calls you now to make your choice—
    To conquer or be slaves:
To meet proud Amanglézi's guns,
    And fight like warriors nobly born:
Or, like Umláo's feeble sons,*
    Become the freeman's scorn.

---

* "Sons of Umláo" is the Caffer name for the Colonial Hottentots.

Then come ye chieftains bold,
   With war plumes waving high;
Come, every warrior, young and old,
   With club and assegai.
Remember how the spoiler's host
   Did through our land like locusts range!
Your herds, your wives, your comrades lost—
   Remember—and revenge!

Fling your broad shields away—
   Bootless against such foes;
But hand to hand we'll fight to-day
   And with their bayonets close.
Grasp each man short his stabbing spear—
   And, when to battle's edge we come,
Rush on their ranks in full career,
   And to their hearts strike home!

Wake! Amakósa, wake!
   And muster for the war:
The wizard-wolves from Keisi's brake,
   The vultures from afar,
Are gathering at Uhlanga's call,
   And follow fast our westward way—
For well they know, ere evening-fall,
   They shall have glorious prey!

Thomas Pringle.

THE INCANTATION.

Half way up Indoda * climbing,
  Hangs the wizard forest old,
From whose shade is heard the chiming
  Of a streamlet clear and cold :
With a mournful sound it gushes
  From its cavern in the steep ;
Then at once its wailing hushes
  In a lakelet dark and deep.

Standing by the dark-blue water,
  Robed in panther's speckled hide,
Who is she ? Jalúhsa's daughter,
  Bold Makanna's widowed bride.
Stern she stands, her left hand clasping
  By the arm her wondering child :
He, her shaggy mantle grasping,
  Gazes up with aspect wild.

Thrice in the soft fount of nursing
  With sharp steel she pierced a vein,—
Thrice the white oppressor cursing,
  While the blood gushed forth amain,—
Wide upon the dark-blue water,
  Sprinkling thrice the crimson tide,—
Spoke Jalúhsa's high-souled daughter,
  Bold Makanna's widowed bride.

---

* Indódo or Indôda Intába, *i.e.*, the Man Mountain, is a conical peaked hill, so called from some resemblance it is supposed to bear to the human figure. It is also known as " Slambie's Kop." It is in the King William's Town District.

THE INCANTATION.

"Thus into the Demon's River
   Blood instead of milk I fling:
Hear, Uhlanga—great Life-Giver!
   Hear, Togúh—Avenging King!
Thus the Mother's feelings tender
   In my breast I stifle now:
Thus I summon you to render
   Vengeance for the Widow's vow!

"Who shall be the Chief's avenger?
   Who the Champion of the Land?
Boy! the pale Son of the Stranger
   Is devoted to *thy* hand.
HE who wields the bolt of thunder
   Witnesses thy Mother's vow!
HE who rends the rocks asunder
   To the task shall train thee now!

"When thy arm grows strong for battle,
   Thou shalt sound Makanna's cry,
Till ten thousand shields shall rattle
   To war-club and assegai:
Then, when like hail-storm in harvest
   On the foe sweeps thy career,
Shall Uhlanga whom thou servest,
   Make them stubble to thy spear!"

Thomas Pringle.

THE CAFFER COMMANDO.

Hark! heard ye the signals of triumph afar?
'Tis our Caffer Commando returning from war:
The voice of their laughter comes loud on the wind,
Nor heed they the curses that follow behind.
For who cares for him, the poor Kósa, that wails
Where the smoke rises dim from yon desolate vales—
That wails for his little ones killed in the fray,
And his herds by the colonist carried away?
Or who cares for him that once pastured this spot,
Where his tribe is extinct and their story forgot?
As many another, ere twenty years pass,
Will only be known by their bones in the grass!
And the sons of the Keisi, the Kei, the Gareep,
With the Gunja and Ghona in silence shall sleep:
For England hath spoke in her tyrannous mood,
And the edict is written in African blood!

Dark Katta * is howling; the eager jackal,
As the lengthening shadows more drearily fall,
Shrieks forth his hymn to the hornèd moon;
And the lord of the desert will follow him soon:
And the tiger-wolf laughs in his bone-strewed brake,
As he calls on his mate and her cubs to awake;
And the panther and leopard come leaping along;
All hymning to Hecate a festival song:
For the tumult is over, the slaughter hath ceased—
And the vulture hath bidden them all to the feast.

Thomas Pringle.

---

* Katberg Mountain.

THE ROCK OF RECONCILEMENT.

A RUGGED mountain, round whose summit proud
The eagle sailed, or heaved the thunder-cloud,
Poured from its cloven breast a gurgling brook,
Which down the grassy glades its journey took;
Oft bending round to lave, with rambling tide,
The groves of evergreens on either side.
Fast by this stream, where yet its course was young,
And, stooping from the heights, the forest flung
A grateful shadow o'er the narrow dell,
Appeared the missionary's hermit cell.
Woven of wattled boughs, and thatched with leaves,
The sweet wild jasmine clustering to its eaves,
It stood, with its small casement gleaming through
Between two ancient cedars. Round it grew
Clumps of acacias and young orange bowers,
Pomegranate hedges, gay with scarlet flowers,
And pale-stemmed fig-trees with their fruit yet green,
And apple blossoms waving light between.
All musical it seemed with humming bees;
And bright-plumed sugar birds among the trees
Fluttered like living blossoms.
       In the shade
Of a grey rock, that 'midst the leafy glade
Stood like a giant sentinel, we found
The habitant of this fair spot of ground—
A plain tall Scottish man, of thoughtful mien;
Grave but not gloomy. By his side was seen
An ancient chief of Amakósa's race,
With javelin armed for conflict or the chase,

And, seated at their feet upon the sod,
A youth was reading from the Word of God,
Of Him who came for sinful men to die,
Of every race and tongue beneath the sky.
Unnoticed, towards them we softly stept.
Our friend was rapt in prayer; the warrior wept,
Leaning upon his hand; the youth read on.
And then we hailed the group: the chieftain's son,
Training to be his country's Christian guide —
And Brownlee and old Ishátshu side by side.

Thomas Pringle.

THE FORESTER OF THE NEUTRAL GROUND.

A SOUTH AFRICAN BORDER BALLAD.

WE met in the midst of the neutral ground,
'Mong the hills where the buffalo's haunts are found;
And we joined in the chase of the noble game,
Nor asked each other of nation or name.

The buffalo bull wheeled suddenly round,
When first from my rifle he felt a wound;
And, before I could gain the Umtóka's bank,
His horns were tearing my courser's flank.

That instant a ball whizzed past my ear,
Which smote the beast in his fierce career;
And the turf was drenched with purple gore,
As he fell at my feet with a bellowing roar.

The stranger came galloping up to my side,
And greeted me with a bold huntsman's pride:
Full blithely we feasted beneath a tree;—
Then out·spoke the Forester, Arend Plessie.

"Stranger, we now are true comrades sworn;
Come pledge me thy hand while we quaff the horn.
Thou'rt an Englishman good, and thy heart is free,
And 'tis therefore I'll tell my story to thee.

"A Heemraad of Camdebóo was my sire;
He had flocks and herds to his heart's desire,
And bondmen and maidens to run at his call,
And seven stout sons to be heirs of all.

"When we had grown up to man's estate,
Our father bid each of us choose a mate,
Of Fatherland blood, from the *black* taint free,
As became a Dutch burgher's proud degree.

"My brothers they rode to the Bovenland,
And each came with a fair bride back in his hand;
But *I* brought the handsomest bride of them all—
Brown Dinah, the bondmaid who sat in our hall.

"My father's displeasure was stern and still;
My brothers' flamed forth like a fire on the hill;
And they said that my spirit was mean and base,
To lower myself to the servile race.

"I bade them rejoice in their herds and flocks,
And their pale-faced spouses with flaxen locks;
While I claimed for my share, as the youngest son,
Brown Dinah alone with my horse and gun.

" My father looked black as a thunder-cloud,
My brothers reviled me and railed aloud,
And their young wives laughed with disdainful pride,
While Dinah in terror clung close to my side.

" Her ebon eyelashes were moistened with tears,
As she shrank abashed from their venomous jeers:
But I bade her look up like a burgher's wife—
Next day to be *mine*, if God granted life.

" At dawn brother Roelof came galloping home
From the pastures—his courser all covered with foam;
''Tis the Bushmen!' he shouted; 'haste friends to the
    spoor!
Bold Arend come help with your long-barrelled roer.'

" Far o'er Bruintjes-hoogtè we followed—in vain:
At length surly Roelof cried, 'Slacken your rein;
We have quite lost the track'—Hans replied with a smile,
—Then my dark-boding spirit suspected their guile.

" I flew to our father's. Brown Dinah was sold!
And they laughed at my rage as they counted the gold.
But I leaped on my horse, with my gun in my hand,
And sought my lost love in the far Bovenland.

" I found her; I bore her from Gauritz' fair glen,
Through lone Zitzikamma, by forest and fen.
To these mountains at last like wild pigeons we flew,
Far, far from the cold hearts of proud Camdebóo.

" I've reared our rude shieling by Gola's green wood,
Where the chase of the deer yields me pastime and food:
With my Dinah and children I dwell here alone,
Without other comrades—and wishing for none.

"I fear not the Bushman from Winterberg's fell,
Nor dread I the Caffer from Kat River's dell;
By justice and kindness I've conquered them both,
And the sons of the desert have pledged me their troth.

"I fear not the leopard that lurks in the wood,
The lion I dread not, though raging for blood;
My hand it is steady—my aim it is sure—
And the boldest must bend to my long-barrelled roer.

"The elephant's buff-coat my bullet can pierce,
And the giant rhinoceros, headlong and fierce;
Gnu, eland, and buffalo furnish my board,
When I feast my allies like an African lord.

"And thus from my kindred and colour exiled,
I live like old Ismael lord of the wild—
And follow the chase with my hounds and my gun,
Nor ever repent the bold course I have run.

"But sometimes there sinks on my spirit a dread
Of what may befall when the turf's on my head;
I fear for poor Dinah—for brown Rodomond
And dimple-faced Karel, the sons of the *bond*.

"Then tell me, dear Stranger, from England the free,
What good tidings bring'st thou for Arend Plessie?
Shall the Edict of Mercy be sent forth at last,
To break the harsh fetters of Colour and Caste?"

Thomas Pringle.

THE EMIGRANT'S CABIN AT THE CAPE.

AN EPISTLE IN RHYME.

WHERE the young river, from its wild ravine,
Winds pleasantly through Eildon's pastures green,—
With fair acacias waving on its banks,
And willows bending o'er in graceful ranks,
And the steep mountain rising close behind,
To shield us from the Snowberg's wintry wind,—
Appears my rustic cabin, thatched with reeds,
Upon a knoll amid the grassy meads;
And, close beside it, looking o'er the lea,
Our summer-seat beneath an umbra-tree.
This morning, musing in that favourite seat,
My hound, old Yarrow, dreaming at my feet,
I pictured you, sage Fairbairn, at my side,
By some good Genie wafted o'er the tide;
And after cordial greetings, thus went on
In fancy's dream our colloquy, dear John.

P.—Enter, my friend, our beehive-cottage door:
No carpet hides the humble earthen floor,
But it is hard as brick, clean-swept and cool.
You must be wearied? Take that jointed stool;
Or on this couch of leopard-skin recline;
You'll find it soft—the workmanship is mine.

F.—Why, Pringle, yes—your cabin's snug enough,
Though oddly shaped. But as for household stuff,
I only see some rough-hewn sticks and spars;
A wicker cupboard, filled with flasks and jars;

A pile of books, on rustic framework placed;
Hides of ferocious beasts that roam the waste;
Whose kindred prowl, perchance, around this spot—
The only neighbours, I suspect, you've got!
Your furniture, rude from the forest cut,
However, is in keeping with the hut.
This couch feels pleasant: is't with grass you stuff it?
So far I should not care with you to rough it.
But—pardon me for seeming somewhat rude—
In this wild place how manage ye for food?

   P.—You'll find, at least, my friend, we do not starve:
There's always mutton, if nought else, to carve;
And even of luxuries we have our share.
And here comes dinner (the best bill of fare)
Drest by that "nut-brown maiden," Vytjè Vaal.
[*To the Hottentot Girl*]. Meid, roep de Juffrowen naar't
     middagmaal.
[*To F.*] Which means—" The ladies into dinner call."

(*Enter Mrs. P. and her Sister, who welcome their Guest to
    Africa. The party take their seats round the table,
    and conversation proceeds.*)

   P.—First, here's our broad-tailed mutton, small and fine,
The dish on which nine days in ten we dine;
Next, roasted springbok, spiced and larded well;
A haunch of hartébeest from Hyndhope Fell;
A paauw, which beats your Norfolk turkey hollow;
Korhaan, and Guinea-fowl, and pheasant follow;
Kid carbonadjes, à-la-Hottentot,
Broiled on a forkèd twig; and, peppered hot
With Chili pods, a dish called Caffer-stew;
Smoked ham of porcupine, and tongue of gnu.

D

This fine white household bread (of Margaret's baking)
Comes from an oven, too, of my own making,
Scooped from an ant-hill. Did I ask before
If you would taste this brawn of forest-boar?

Our fruits, I must confess, make no great show:
Trees, grafts, and layers must have time to grow.
But there's green roasted maize, and pumpkin pie,
And wild asparagus. Or will you try
A slice of water-melon?—fine for drouth,
Like sugared ices melting in the mouth.
Here too are wild grapes from our forest-vine,
Not void of flavour, though unfit for wine.
And here comes dried fruit I had quite forgot,
(From fair Glen-Avon, Margaret, is it not?)
Figs, almonds, raisins, peaches. Witbooy Swart
Brought this huge sackful from kind Mrs. Hart—
Enough to load a Covent-Garden cart.

But come, let's crown the banquet with some wine,
What will you drink? Champagne? Port? Claret? Stein?
Well—not to tease you with a thirsty jest,
Lo, there our *only* vintage stands confest,
In that half-aum upon the spigot-rack.
And, certes, though it keeps the old *kaap smaak*,
The wine is light and racy; so we learn,
In laughing mood, to call it Cape Sauterne.
—Let's pledge this cup " to all our friends," Fairbairn!

F.—Well, I admit, my friend, your dinner's good.
Springbok and porcupine are dainty food;
That lordly paauw was roasted to a turn;
And, in your country fruits, and Cape Sauterne,

The wildish flavour's really—not unpleasant;
And I may say the same of gnu and pheasant.
—But—Mrs. Pringle ... shall I have the pleasure ... ?
Miss Brown, ... some wine?—(These quaighs are quite
   a treasure)
—What! leave us now? I've much to ask of *you* ...
But since you *will* go—for an hour adieu.
                              [*Exeunt Ladies.*

But, Pringle—"à nos moutons revenons"—
Cui bono's still the burden of my song—
Cut off, with these good ladies, from society,
Of savage life you soon must feel satiety:
The MIND requires fit exercise and food,
Not to be found 'mid Afric's desert rude.
And what avail the spoils of wood and field,
The fruits or vines your fertile valleys yield,
Without that higher zest to crown the whole—
"The feast of Reason and the flow of Soul?"
—Food, shelter, fire, suffice for savage men;
But can the comforts of your wattled den,
Your sylvan fare and rustic tasks suffice
For one who once seemed finer joys to prize?
—When, erst, like Virgil's swains, we used to sing
Of streams and groves, and "all that sort of thing,"
The spot we meant for our "poetic den"
Was always within reach of books and men;
By classic Esk, for instance, or Tweed-side,
With gifted friends within an easy ride;
Besides our college chum, the parish priest;
And the said den with six good rooms at least.—
Here! save for her who shares and soothes your lot,
You might as well squat in a Caffer's cot!

Come, now, be candid: tell me, my dear friend,
Of your aspiring aims is *this* the end?
Was it for nature's wants, fire, shelter, food,
You sought this dreary, soulless solitude?
Broke off your ties with men of cultured mind,
Your native land, your early friends resigned?
As if, believing with insane Rousseau
Refinement the chief cause of human woe,
You meant to realise that raver's plan,
And be a philosophic *Bosjesman!*—
Be frank; confess the fact you cannot hide—
You sought this den from disappointed pride.

P.—You've missed the mark, Fairbairn: my breast is
    clear.
Nor wild romance nor pride allured me here:
Duty and destiny with equal voice
Constrained my steps: I had no other choice.
    The hermit "lodge in some vast wilderness,"
Which sometimes poets sigh for, I confess,
Were but a sorry lot. In real life
One needs a friend—the best of friends, a wife:
But with a home thus cheered, however rude,
There's nought so very dull in solitude,—
Even though that home should happen to be found,
Like mine, in Africa's remotest bound.
—I have my farm and garden, tools and pen;
My schemes for civilising savage men;
Our Sunday service, till the Sabbath-bell
Shall wake its welcome chime in Lynden dell:
Some duty or amusement, grave or light,
To fill the active day from morn till night:

And thus two years so lightsomely have flown
That still we wonder when the week is gone.
—We have at times our troubles, it is true,
Passing vexations and privations too;
But were it not for woman's tender frame,
These are annoyances I scarce would name;
For though perchance they plague us while they last,
They only serve for jests when they are past.

And then your notion that we're *quite* exiled
From social life amid these mountains wild,
Accords not with the fact—as you will see
On glancing o'er this district map with me.

. . . . . .

Thomas Pringle.

THE VOLUNTEERS OF ENGLAND.

BY A COLONIST.

Cælum non animum mutant qui trans mare currunt.

A TRUMPET blast is pealing
   'Mongst Albion's echoing hills,
Arousing every feeling
   That patriot's bosom thrills:
O'er hill and dale resounding,
   It sends its loud alarm;
The Freeman's war-cry sounding,—
   " For Hearths and Altars, arm!"

A Despot's monster legions
  Are on their haughty way;
A Despot's warlike regions
  Send forth their proud array,
To raze the broad foundations
  Of Freedom's Temple shrine,
And from among the nations
  To blot her name divine.

From peasant's lowly dwelling;
  From baron's ancient hall,
With bosoms proudly swelling,
  Rise! sons of England, ALL!
From Cambria's vales of beauty,
  "Britons" of Britain, come,
Prompt at the call of duty,
  With strong right arm "strike home!"

From every mist-clad mountain,
  Sons of the hardy North,
From lake, and glen, and fountain,
  Come in your manhood forth.
From Eastern fen and plainland,
  From Western tarn and fell,
From islet, rock, and mainland
  The nation's gathering swell.

"WE COME!" in tones of thunder,
  Rings echoing round the land;
"We come!" and scenes of wonder
  Burst forth on every hand.

Workmen have sprung to warriors,
   Herdsmen to heroes grown,
And rise, in living barriers,
   Around VICTORIA's throne.

Peasant and peer are joining,
   Yeoman with baron stands;
Strength, wealth, and rank combining,
   And nerving hearts and hands.
Loyal, if "horny-handed,"
   Industry's thousands come;
In brother's compact banded
   For Altar, Throne, and Home.

Hear it! to Heaven ascending,
   A nation's solemn vow;
While, at His altar bending,
   To God *alone* they bow.
" No foreign Home invading,
   We strike no foreign throne;
But,—God from Heaven aiding,
   To *death* we guard OUR OWN."

Rev. H. H. Dugmore.

July 2, 1861.

"THE DEAR OLD LAND."

A GLORIOUS land is the "Dear Old Land,"
   Our fathers' island home;
Tho' its moorlands are cold when the snow lies deep,
And the mists round the sides of its mountains creep,
And the waves are white when the March winds sweep,
   As they dash on its cliffs in foam.

'Tis changed since the days when the Druid old
    Was seen in the forest glades;
When the wolf was tracked to his mountain den,
And the wild boar roused in the gloomy glen,
And the chase was a sport to test the *men*
    That ranged through the leafy shades.

Where the victim bled on the altar stone,
    Or died in a fiery grave;—
Where wild woods sheltered the outlaw's band,—
Where the salt marsh mingled sea and land,
Proud mansions rise, or cities stand,
    Or golden harvests wave.

A story of fame has the "Dear Old Land,"
    And it dates from the days gone by;
When Right with Might the strife began,
And Freedom's voice with the Fire-cross ran,
And the wakened Serf rose up,—a MAN,
    To conquer his rights, or DIE!

There were hardy souls in the "Dear Old Land,"
    In the stern dark days of yore,
When the arm could *do* what the heart could *dare*,
And the threats of a tyrant were "empty air,"
And they made him tremble in his lair,
    As they roused themselves in power.

A story of fame has the "Dear Old Land,"
    And it is not ended yet.
Wherever the sea's wild waves have curled
Her fleets proudly sail with flag unfurled,
And many a lesson they've taught the world,
    Which the world will not forget.

And tell me the land, o'er the earth's broad face,
    Where her "braves" have not been found,
From East to West, with the glorious sun,
The sound of their drums when the day is done,
From realm to realm goes rolling on
    Unceasing the wide world round!

   .   .   .   .

But the warrior's fame has stains of blood,
    And it raises the widow's wail;
Look we then on the glories whose milder rays
Will bring no tears to the eyes that gaze;
Whose trophies of triumph, whose songs of praise
    The tenderest heart may hail.

There are spirits of *might* in the "Dear Old Land,"
    That have seized on a giant grim,
And the burdens which man and beast had borne
With sweat of brow, and frame hard worn
From morn till night, and from night till morn,
    They have boldly laid on *him*.

He raises the load from the deep dark mine,
    He speeds the loom amain;
He wields the ponderous hammer's force,
Gives the ship 'gainst wind and tide free course,
And snorts in the breath of the iron horse
    That nor weariness feels, nor pain.

'Tis glorious to ride at his headlong pace
    'Mongst the crags of the forest glen,
To skim o'er the moorlands bleak and wide,

To pierce through the rock-ribbed mountain side,
As he *plays* with the work—in giant pride—
   Of twice ten thousand men.

There are spirits of *power* in the " Dear Old Land,"
   Who can bid the lightning speed
From North to South, from East to West,—
A courier swift that asks no rest,
But instant writes command or quest
   Where the " ends of the world " may read.

There are spirits of *light* in the " Dear Old Land,"
   Who rejoice when "the Truth makes free ;"
Who shout when a nation wakes in might,
And seizes its long denied birth-*right*,
And prisoned *souls* burst forth to light ;—
   O, glorious sight to see !

There are spirits of *love* in the " Dear Old Land,"
   Who weep for their kindred's wrongs ;
And who *work* as they weep, in patient power,
Through the livelong day,—through the midnight hour
While rescued victims blessings shower
   From wondering, grateful tongues.

Then hail ! all hail ! thou " Dear Old Land,"
   Where our fathers' ashes lie ;
There are sunbeams bright on this far off shore,
There are starlit skies when the day is o'er,—
And we never shall tread thy greensward more,
   But we'll love thee,—TILL WE DIE !

Rev. H. H. Dugmore.

THE FUNERAL IN THE ABBEY.

LIST! there is music sounding!
Not airy strains, that lead the mazy dance;
Not trumpet tones, that stir the warrior's soul;
But soft, and slow, and solemn, as it swells
And rolls afar and dies, midst its own echoes
From vaulted roof, and lofty aisle dim-lighted,
Where clustering columns rise, and rainbow rays
Gleam in their varied glory o'er the scene.
  'Tis in the sacred fane where sleeps the dust
Of those whom Britain loves to honour, who
Shed living honour by their deeds on *her*,
Challenging place upon the rolls of Fame.
Sages, and saints, and sons of song lie there;
Wresters of Nature's secrets;—senators,
Whose thund'rous eloquence could awe the world;
Patriots whose lifeblood for their country flowed;
War chiefs who led her armies on to glory;
Statesmen with eye far-reaching, who could thread
Diplomacy's dark mazes, and, the helm
With firm hand grasping, steer the nation's bark
Through storms of strife to honour and to peace.
  And royalty's proud dust lies mouldering there,
'Neath sculptured marbles, or midst gilded shrines:
While high o'erhead the ancient banners droop.—
Monarchs of other days,—of other *ages*,
Successive generations of the great,
Who ruled the realm of England as *she* grew
From isolate obscurity to greatness
That with a fame undying fills the world.

Lo! *there*,—an open grave! and heads are bare,
And bent;—and bosoms heave, and tears are falling
From youthful womanhood,—from hoary age.
Men weep, as slowly through the reverent throng
Is borne what hides from view a shrivelled form,
Wasted and featureless: yet round that bier
Stand silently the great of many lands.
Britain's high-born stand there; and kings of men
Of other realms stand there by envoy.   There
The sons of science gather, and the friends
Of light and liberty.   The Churches' messengers
Look on in sadness there; and a vast throng,
Crowding around, sigh forth a *nation's* sympathy.

Tokens of reverent love,—azalea wreaths,
Laurel and myrtle, with fair flowers entwined,
Bright immortelles, branches of Afric's palm,—
(Symbol of triumph e'en in death) are there.
And,—honour to the honour'd!—Britain's Queen
Sign of "respect and admiration" sends,—
Her own, and royal daughter's funeral gifts
To deck the bier.
                  And *who* is it that thus
Draws to himself, in *death*, the eyes of nations?
Is it some warrior leader, who has died
In the proud hour of victory; and, wept
By a whole people's tears, lies down to rest?
—Or is it one who, in a nation's peril,
Has earned a nation's gratitude by wise
And warning counsels in her council halls?
—Is it a *Prince* has died?   That royalty
Should sigh her grief, and nobles weep around?

'Tis LIVINGSTONE!—That name a thousand tongues

Through years of hope and fear alternate, uttered;
While he who bore it, deep in Afric's wilds,
Solving her mystery of ages, trod
Her deserts, traced her streams,—a pioneer
Of science, commerce, liberty, and mercy.
—A "weaver boy" thus honoured!—Wherefore *not*?
He wore, indeed, no ducal coronet;
Nor dwelt in lordly hall. But "stamp" of "rank"*
He needed not, while Nature's "gold" of manhood,
Solid, and pure, and bright, shone through his soul.

 The "weaver boy," in youthful prime, had yearned
O'er Afric's sons enslaved; for his *own* soul,
By "grace of God" emancipated, longed
To free from bondage "body, soul, and spirit"
Of those who were immortal as himself,
And co-redeemed, though dark in mind as hue.
 He bore the Cross's standard o'er the plains
Where wandering tribes by MOFFAT gathered dwelt;
And preached the Cross's story in the tongues
Strange to his earlier years.—But as he stood,
And looked to "regions" yet "beyond," where white
  man's foot
Had never trod, *fresh* longings filled his soul.
—"Millions dwell yonder:—all unknown to us,
They live and die in darkness: and they groan
In bitter bondage, where no ray of hope
Shines through the gloom.—I go to find the way:—
Let others follow."
    And he went,—alone;
And braved the desert blast, the serpent's folds,

---

* Burns.

The jungle's ambush, and the lion's fang:
He braved the fevered swamp, the tropic sun,
The mountain torrent, and the savage spear.
Barbarian wonder followed in his steps;
And treachery shrank before the magic power
Of Christian kindness, single and unarmed.
He vanished from our sight,—and time rolled on
While he was lost from view.
                        At length was heard
Rumour of strange discoveries: lakes unknown
Had spread their silver waters to his gaze;
And mighty streams, through vales all green and glorious
Poured their vast floods o'er thundering cataracts,
Where men had deemed were nought but deserts drear.
  "From ocean through to ocean" tropic realms
Were traversed with unfaltering footsteps, till
Regions before unknown, with all their wonders
Rose into view, and hidden tribes disclosed
Their being and their need.
                        He rested then
Awhile, and told his countrymen the story
Of his lone wanderings over Afric's wilds.
Men wondered while they listened, as they heard
Of grassy slopes, and waving woods, and sparkling waters;
Of birds of beauty, flowers of gorgeous hues;
And these where they had pictured a Sahara,
With 'whelming sandstorms, and the death-blast dire
Of red simoom.
                        He rested not for long:—
The spell 'was on him, and his work not done.
  And now he led a band, who bore the light
Of truth divine, to chase away the darkness
That brooded over regions bright and fair,

Where "man alone is vile."—'Twas there he laid
The partner of his bosom, who had shared
The joys and sorrows of his younger years.
A grave by Shire's Waters, far away
From home and kindred, holds the precious dust.

And now his ties to earth are loosened:—now,
The beckoning Hand that calls him onwards still,
Is seen more plainly,—and he follows. He
Would lift the cloud from regions still unknown;
Heard of but through the victims of a vile
Traffic in human blood. His soul was fired
With ardent resolution to destroy,
(Or perish in the contest) the dire curse
That blighted nations when they might be blest.

A vision rose before him:—These fair realms
Yielding earth's teeming increase in exchange
For varied handiwork of other lands;—
An open-handed commerce giving boons
To honest industry, while *crushing down*
The cursed manstealer's trade:—The light of truth,
Of *Christian* truth, for mind, and heart, and life,
For family and nation, blending with
Prismatic rays by science shed around:
The darkness melting, heathen orgies vile
Yielding the place to worship bright and pure;
Songs of salvation where the savage yells;—
Slavery of mind and body killed together,
And Freedom smiling glad o'er all the land!
—This was his vision;—and it might be *true;*—
And he would *labour* that it might,—to *death!*

Again, yet once again, the word, "Farewell!"
A *last* farewell: we heard his voice no more.
The years rolled on,—and on: he came not back.
Tidings, indeed, there were; but "far between,
Like angel visits," were those tidings brief,
That still he lived, and toiled,—the white man lone,
Who with such wondrous spell o'er savage minds,
And with charmed life, held pain and death at bay.
—And then came silence.——"Has he sunk *at last?*"
And then came *other* tidings;—"He is *dead!*
And dead by murderous hands!"—And hearts were chilled
With horror, and stood still.—But some said, "No!
Not *thus* will that brave spirit pass away.
Africa *knows* his errand:—'tis *not* so."
Nor was it so. A kindred spirit sought,
And *found* him!—and with all the old fire burning;
But with the *censer* now well nigh consumed.
—"Come home with me, and *rest:* well hast thou earned
The right upon thy laurels to repose:—
The *world* is yearning o'er thee:—Come and *rest!*"

"Not yet! not yet! There is *still* work to do.
Let me but show the way to Afric's *heart:*—
Leave me to trace the water-path by which
Old England's white-wing'd sea-birds shall ascend,—
Bearing her light, and liberty, and peace,—
To roll away the dark reproach of ages;
And *then*,—MY WORK IS DONE."

And STANLEY left him.

And then, th' enfeebled frame, once more essaying
To climb the mountain, pierce the forest's gloom,

Stem the swift torrent, cross the lake's broad breast,
And wade the sedgy marsh,—*gave way at last!*
But still the spirit, o'er the flesh triumphant,
Registered till the "hand had lost its cunning,"
The record precious of that life's last task,
Which only death could end. . . .
He died alone: none saw the spirit part.
Thus had he willed to die;—*alone with* GOD.
   The morning greeting of his faithful band
No longer met the welcome, kind response.
The spirit had gone *home;* and gone in silence;—
And there knelt lifeless clay!
                                     And none were nigh,
Save Afric's swarthy sons. But these had learned
To love and reverence him whose *life* was given
A sacrifice for injured Afric's weal;
And they would guard his relics, e'en in death.
   They left his *heart* where *fitly* it should rest;
And bore, in reverent hands, the faded form,
Rudely, but lovingly embalmed; and after days,
And weeks, and *months*, of weary toil,
Gave to its kindred their last sacred trust;—
And *there* it lies!—and thousands stand around,
To do the martyr honour as he rests.

   And now "his body" sinks from mortal sight,
Midst showers of amaranths, and fragrant flowers,
That, white and pure, fall fast from loving hands.
"Buried in peace," it lies, 'mongst kindred heroes:
While white-robed choristers, and organ pealing,
Blend in the final, loud, triumphant strain,
And the high arches echo as they sing,—
"But his soul *liveth!* LIVETH EVERMORE!"

Rev. H. H. *Dugmore.*

STORMBERG, *May* 1874.

A FAREWELL TO ENGLISH FRIENDS.

"Far, far away!"
Simple, but sadly tender,
These words unlock the heart's deep springs
  And bid its fountains play.
What thoughts upon the spirit rush!
What feelings from the warm heart gush,
While we pause to think on those we love,
  Now far, far away!

Far, far away!
We shall think on "happy England,"
And many a "sunny memory" will shed its golden ray,
  And many a welcome and farewell
  From unforgotten lips will dwell
  Like music's echoes in our minds
    When far, far away.

Far, far away!
While our sails are proudly swelling,
While the breezes bear us onward, and the wild waves
  round us play,
While *our* prayers rise to heaven above,
And ask its care for those we love,
Think on *us*,—pray for *us*,
  The "Far, far away!"

Far, far away!
For "Afric's sunny fountains"
Our seabird spreads her snowy wings
  Midst ocean's sparkling spray;

Old England's shores are fading fast;
One look! the fondest, and the *last;*
For we go to DIE in distant realms
    Far, far away!

A MISSIONARY'S LAST FAREWELL TO ENGLAND.

LAND of my birth, farewell! Thy shores are fading
In the dark distance, and the ocean's waves
Are hiding thee from view; while, sadly aiding
To dim my vision of thy snowy cliffs,
My tears unbidden start. O happy land!
I did not know how much I loved thee, till
The breezes bore me from thee, and I gazed
A long last look.   I left thee when a child;
And Afric's summer suns full forty years
Have burned upon my head, since in thy groves
My boyish footsteps wandered. But my heart
Was yet unwithered, and could quiver still
When sounded on my ear thy name of glory.

While oceans rolled between us, in my dreams
My thoughts were of thee: but in waking hours
I scarcely dared to hope to see thee more.
I lingered o'er the story of thy fame,
And joyed to claim thee as my native isle;
A day-star to the nations, that would fain
Follow, though from afar, thy track of light,
And in its beams find their own way to freedom.

In the far solitudes of regions dark
With heathen gloom, my pensive soul has mused,
And I have sighed to sun me in the light
Which long has been thy halo; light from heaven,
Amidst the brightness of whose gladdening rays
Thy temples, halls, and palaces have stood
Irradiate. But it might not, could not be.

At length I saw thee once again! and then
How thrilled my very heart-core as thy coasts
Loomed through the mists of morning on my view,
And thy proud vision of historic glory
Marched in its dioramic grandeur past!
I leaped upon thy freeborn soil once more:
Thy fields were laughing, glad with spring-tide flowers,
Thy greenwoods waving in the fresh wind's breath;
Thy streams, bounding from winter's cold embrace,
Threaded the vales with silver; while I stood
And gazed with rapture, fresh and pure as boyhood's,
In 'wildering ecstasy. And then I swept
On steam-wings o'er thy plains, and round thy hills,
And down thy vales, 'mongst beauty ever changing:
Now looking on the cornfield's waving gladness;
Now drinking fragrance from the hayfield's breath;
Now wondering like a child, as ivied towers,
And slender church-spires, from their sheltering groves
Pointing to heaven, and old baronial halls,
Standing apart amidst their dark woods' pride,
And crumbling castle-keeps, that tell of times
When warders blew their horns, and mailèd knights
Broke spears and shattered helms in tournament,
As these, and thousand more, went sailing by:
Till plunged at last amidst the 'whelming tide

Of thy great city's life, I sank, a drop,
Into its vast and restless ocean-whirl.

  .   .   .   .   .   .

But is it so?　And I have really trod
Thy soil again?　Or did I only *dream?*
Methought I mingled with thy multitudes,
And saw the swarms of thy industrial hives
Plying their ceaseless task, and piling stores
To meet the wide world's wants.　Methought I saw
Thy quickened life-blood of commercial being
Pour through its iron veins the vital stream,
Infusing universal energy.
Did not thy glorious structures rise before me—
Houses of mercy, halls and kingly courts?
Did not imperial Windsor glad my eyes,
Where England's banner, free and proud, was waving;
Brother-like greeting the free winds of heaven?
Did I not wander through the gorgeous halls
Where England's senators, in trumpet tones,
Have poured forth eloquence that awed the world?
Where, mildly ruling, sits a mother Queen,—
Her real throne a nation's loving heart.
Have I not stood within thy sacred fanes,
Listening entranced, as billowing music rolled,
And distant, broke upon the sculptured stone
Like ocean's waves upon their rocky bounds?
And—tenderer, dearer recollection still—
My mother's and my childhood's humble home,
With childhood's memories clustering thick around it:
Did I not stand again upon its threshold,
And greet my childhood's playmates?　Ah! how
 changed!

Or was all this a dream? A happy dream,
That rose in brightness, and then passed away
For ever? No! It was not all a dream.
The welcome of warm hearts was *real*, and then
The glow of friendships formed was no illusion.
Men great and good have spoken sacred truth;
And I have listened with enraptured ears,
As eloquence of Heaven's own kindling burst
In burning power from consecrated lips.
And I have seen the Church's standard-bearers:
Men, crowned in hoary age with silver glory,
Have blessed me in the Master's sacred name,
And bidden me God-speed in God's great service.
And I have mingled with the throngs that sent
Up to high heaven their swelling song of praise,
That, as "the voice of many waters," rose
Exultant from the lips and hearts of thousands,
When the glad tidings came that "God was raised
Up from His holy habitation" and
Was pouring forth His Spirit on the nations.

I did not dream when I beheld the light
Of holy rapture beam from thousand eyes:
I was not dreaming when I shared the glow
Of wondering gratitude with thousand hearts.
And when our "Hallelujah" rent the skies,
And our rapt spirits felt the bliss of heaven
Descend to meet us in the golden cloud
Of God's own presence, 'twas a glorious truth,
A joy to feed the soul upon for ever!

And yet 'tis like a dream: for, scarcely seen,
Thy beauties fade from view; and the rich notes,

That thrilled the soul to rapture, thrill no more.
'Twas but a glimpse of glory,—and 'tis gone.
'Twas but a taste of joy that left the soul
Hungering with keener appetite.   I go
Just as my spirit is awaking, quick
With new strange life and feeling; just
As awakens fresh the home-throb of my heart,
Owning its English birth.
      Well, be it so!
'Tis God that bids me go; 'tis duty calls
Back to the land of darkness.   Be it so!
'Tis well that I should go, ere silken webs,
Woven by Christian kindness round my heart,
Become too strong to leave me power to rend them.
I go, to look upon thee never more;
I go, but breathing prayers and blessings on thee.

O England, speck amidst the world of waters!
Thou art the world's great wonder.   Realms afar
Have heard thy voice, have seen thy light, have felt
  thy power.
Some, jealous, envy thee; some bless thy name,
The might of freedom, and the light of truth,—
The freedom that can burst the *spirit's* bonds,
The light that leads that spirit up to heaven,—
These are thy charge, and for the wide world's weal,
Be faithful to thy trust, thou honour'd Isle!
Thou hast a glorious mission to the nations.
Hold fast the truth of God with strong right hand,
Cast forth the traitors that would " take thy crown."
Still send thy sons, as Mercy's angels, forth
To sound in silver tones, to far-off lands,
The trumpet of the everlasting gospel;

So shall Heaven's smile be thy perpetual light,
And Heaven's dread power, "a wall of fire," thy guard.

. . . . . .

And now 'tis past ! nor faintest trace remains
Of headland, cliff, or mountain in the line
Of the far off horizon ; and in vain
I strain my aching sight to catch one glimpse,
But one glimpse more.   England, farewell !
Island of beauty, changing not with seasons ;
Island of glory, dimming not with years ;
Isle rich in blessings strewn by God's own hand,—
My native Isle !   A fond long last farewell !

Rev. H. H. Dugmore.

ENGLISH CHANNEL, *October* 9, 1859.

A REMINISCENCE OF 1820.

IN the lone wilderness behold them stand,
Gazing with new strange feelings on the scenes
Now spread around them in a foreign clime,
Far from the sea-girt home that gave them birth.

They had been landed on a cheerless shore,
Dreary and solitary ; and the hope
That erst had brightened all their visions, when,
O'er the blue waters looming from afar,
They had seen Afric's mountains rise to view,
Had nigh been quenched again.   But they had left

The barren strand, and over hill and dale
Had slowly toiled to reach a place of rest,
And give their children once again a home.

Men roughly kind, of speech and manners strange,
Had guided them ; and bidding them farewell,
Had left them houseless in the wilderness,
Pitying, and wondering what their fate might be.
Fathers and mothers, with their children round them,
Stand on the green sward, while the sunny skies,
Flecked with bright clouds, bend o'er them from above,
And thoughts are far away o'er the wide waters.
The parting scene comes back to memory's view,—
The last embrace of loved ones left behind,
The fears, and hopes, and prayers of that sad hour.

And now the little ones in thoughtless glee
Chase the bright butterflies of this strange land,—
Their new and untried home. Ah! 'twas for *them*
The fathers braved the storm-tossed waters, and
The mothers hushed their own alarms to peace,
When the loud tempest howled around the bark
That bore them onward o'er the surging waves.
These gave the springs to their great enterprise,
And broke the bonds that else had held them still
In the old home circle of the Fatherland.

Dark days had been in England. Darker still
Seemed coming fast, and o'er the crowded throngs
Of Britain's cities, stern adversity
Was frowning. Then the cry arose,
"What of our *children* ? What awaits *them* here ?
Must we look on, and see their budding life,

Before it blossoms, wither in our sight?
Are there not other lands where pining want
Shall cease to mock at honest industry,
That asks but leave to labour? Will no star
Of hope arise to point to happier climes
Where skies are not *all* dark? Be it to rend
The ties of kindred, we must venture forth
Over the unknown seas, and seek a home
On foreign shores, where there is room to live,
And light to see a future for our children,
Happy and bright when *we* have sunk to rest."

And this is now their home.
                    'Tis lone and wild;
But there is beauty in its wildness. See!
Yonder are mountains; in their deep ravines
Dark woods are waving, whence in noisy flight ,
Wild parrots issue forth, while loories hide
Amidst their deep recesses. Water springs
Send limpid streamlets down the mountain side,
Fringed with bright evergreens, and brighter flowers.

Issuing from yonder dark and craggy gorge,
Where lurks the stealthy leopard, and where shouts
With loudly echoing voice the bold baboon,
Kareiga winds its devious course along
Between its willowed banks; while here and there
The dark-leaved yellow wood lifts its proud head
In stately dignity. Along the vale
The wildwood's sheltering covert stretches, where
The bushbok barks; the duiker, sudden, springs;
The timid bluebok through the moonlight glides;
And monkey mimics chatter saucily.

And there are feathered songsters in the groves;
Not with the thrush's or the blackbird's notes,
That flood Old England's woods with melody;
But short, and sharp, and ringing in their tones,
Responsive to each other from afar,
While telling of a life of light and joy.

In the green pastures on the sunny slopes,
Where the mimosa's golden blossoms shed
Gales of perfume around; and fertile soils
Promise the husbandman a rich return
To cheer him in his toil.
                      "This is our home!
A spot on earth we now can call *our own;*
A starting-point for a new life's career.
Wake all our energies afresh! A brighter day
Has dawned at last upon us. Let us raise
A song of gratitude to Heaven,
And gird us for our duties."

PAST AND PRESENT.

OVER the waters wide and deep
Where the storm-waves roll, and the storm-winds sweep,—
Over the waters see them come!
Breasting the billows' curling foam,
Fathers for children seeking a home
              In Afric's Southern Wilds.

Wilderness lands of brake and glen,
The wolf's and the panther's gloomy den;—

Wilderness plains where the springbok bounds,
And the lion's voice from the hill resounds,—
And the vulture circles in airy rounds,
   Are Afric's Southern Wilds.

"Hand to the labour!—heart and hand!
Our sons shall inherit an altered land:
Harvests shall wave o'er the virgin soil,
Cottages stand, and gardens smile,
And the songs of our children the hours beguile,
   'Mid Afric's Southern Wilds.

"Make we the pride of the forest yield;
Wrest from the wilderness field on field;
And to brighten our hope, and lighten our care,
And gain the aid of our Father there,
Raise we to heaven the voice of prayer
   From Afric's Southern Wilds."

 . . . . . .

The locust clouds have darkened heaven;
The "rusted" fields to the flame are given:
The war-cry is echoing wild and loud;
For the war of the savage, fierce and proud,
Has burst like the storm from the thunder-cloud
   On Afric's Southern Wilds.

"*Never despair*, though the harvests fail;
Though the hosts of a savage foe assail;
Never despair; we shall conquer yet,
And the toils of our earlier years forget
In hope's bright glory our sun shall set
   'Midst Afric's Southern Wilds."

 . . . .

Our toilworn fathers are sinking to rest;
But their children inherit their hope's bequest.
Valleys are smiling in harvest pride;
There are fleecy flocks on the mountain side;
Cities are rising to stud the plains;
The life-blood of commerce is coursing the veins
Of a new-born Empire, that grows and reigns
    Over Afric's Southern Wilds.

Rev. H. H. Dugmore.

April 10, 1861.

A SOUTH AFRICAN WILDERNESS.

The wilderness! The wilderness! It stretches wide and drear,
As I stand amidst its solitudes with no companion near:
I watch the vulture sailing as he circles in the sky,
The ostrich stalking o'er the wilds—the springbok bounding by.

The wilderness! The wilderness! 'Tis where the lion roars;
And whence the wasting locust-flood its living torrent pours:
With rushing ruin on their wings, its myriad myriads sweep,
Like waters from the mountains, or the surges of the deep.

The wilderness! The wilderness! The desert blast is there;
And the sun sends down his fiery rays with fierce and blinding glare.

'Tis there the infant whirlwinds their new-born vigour try;
And spiral columns o'er the waste rise circling to the sky.

There gathering vultures' sounding wings swoop on their hapless prey;
And they clamour round their victim ere life has ebbed away.
The "ringhals" rises on his coil at the startled traveller's side;
The false mirage's wavy streams in phantom ripples glide.

Strange sounds are in the wilderness: the wild dog's plaintive wail,
As he calls his fellows from afar, comes faintly on the gale.
The vulture's voice screams harshly, as he sights his prey on high;
The bursting meteor echoes from the regions of the sky.

A thousand insect voices, with their thousand notes are there;
With chirrup, ring, or buzz of wing, they fill the sounding air;
And waking fancy starts to hear the trumpet's note afar;
The pibroch's martial gathering, the barbarian's cry of war.

But the wilderness has lessons: in danger's lonely hour,
How weak man's solitary arm! How vain his boast of power!
The humbled spirit learns to look for Heaven's protecting care;
Is *safety* in the wilderness? Then God is present there.

The wilderness might wean the heart from earth and
    earthly love ;
And bid the freed affections soar to happier realms above.
Look now upon this barren waste, then turn thy wistful
    eyes
To the fields where flowers immortal bloom, beyond the
    starry skies.

No scorching sun, no withering wind, no serpent's tooth
    is there :
No vulture swoop of terror; no locust-cloud of care.
No faithless mocking phantom-streams the longing eyes
    beguile ;
But living fountains sparkle bright in God's eternal smile.

Rev. H. H. Dugmore.

A SUNRISE THOUGHT AT "COVE ROCK."

KING of the Golden Orient :—lo ! he comes
And mounts, magnificent, his burning throne ;
Smiling in glory o'er the world of waters,
Whose joyous waves leap welcome to his coming.
See how the streaming rays, his almoners,
Fling forth his largesses in flashing brilliants.
Which the waves catch, and toss from crest to crest
In dancing rapture ! 'Tis a glorious sight
To see a king right welcome to his subjects ;
To hear the voice of gladness universal
Greeting his royal smile. Not sea *alone,*
But ocean, earth, and sky join look and voice

In smile and song. See there in the far west,
Where little cloudlets cluster, as they hang
In modest diffidence upon the outskirts
Of the vast audience-throng: they too are flushing
Bright with the universal joy:—and hark!
Breezes are striking their Æolian harps
Among the woods that wave along the hills;
While the deep voices of the surge, far pealing,
Thunder their ceaseless anthem to his praise.

    Brief, as befitting, is the monarch's audience;
For who may look upon the King of light
With eye unblenching? Now in massy folds,
The darkening curtains of his cloud pavilion
Gather around him;—and though dazzling still
Their broad gold fringes wave, the weak eye rests
From his transpiercing glance of *unveiled* glory.

    Hail! glorious image of the KING OF KINGS!
Seen or unseen, thou givest light, and life,
And joy, and beauty to revolving worlds
That circle round thy throne. Centre of power!
Thy mystery of might upholds, sustains,
And governs as the Delegate of God,
Their measured harmony of ceaseless motion;
Reining their fleetness with "an arm of strength"
Felt and obeyed in the far depths of space,
Where roll remotest planets round their spheres
In twilight solitude, unseen, unknown.

Rev. H. H. Dugmore.

AN OCEAN SUNSET.

'Tis sunset on the ocean! Let us gaze:—
A Sabbath sunset; and all things combine
To give it peace and beauty; for the winds
Have folded their broad pinions, and have sunk
To peaceful slumber on the ocean's breast—
The sportive waves, that tossed their spray erewhile,
Displume their crests in reverence for the hour,
And all is calm around.   The curtain cloud
That hung o'er all the west throws wide its folds,
And in the clear blue ether far away
Bright islands of the blest seem floating, free
From the rough cares that fret this lower world,
And radiant in a glory all divine.

Are not our long-lost loved ones hov'ring there,
Can we not see them wave their hands of light,
As if to beckon to their bright abodes?
Are not celestial harp-strings sounding? Oh!
Let glad imagination spread her wings,
And soar to catch the echoes of their songs
Ere the ethereal vision fades away.

Hail to a scene that wakens thoughts like these.
'Tis sweet to rise, though but on *fancy's* wing,
And antedate communion with the blest,
For Heaven is *real!* May its magnet power
Touch every point of vision! till the soul,
Drawn by a might resistless, *centres there!*

A SIGHT FROM THE SHORE.

I LOOK upon the ocean.   Far away,
A fleet of thunder-clouds is sailing by.
High in mid heaven the aërial canvas swells,
And proudly scorns the breeze's proffered aid;
Instinct with its own spirit's breath of life,
That bears it onward in its majesty:
While ever and anon the signal flash
From van, and rear, and centre, tells of might
Resistless.   Stern, and slow, and dark, and grand,
Its shadows sweep o'er ocean's heaving billows;
While avant couriers, on the lightning's wing,
Herald its coming to the distant realms
Beyond the horizon's verge.

THE THUNDERSTORM AT BATHURST.

'TWAS eve; but 'twas not as it oft had been,
When the sun, ere he sank from the lovely scene,
Had smiled in glory o'er mount and dale,
And the forest gloom, and the cloudlet pale,
And the verdant lawn, and the flow'ret gay,
Were tinged with the gold of his parting ray.
While sweet was the breath of the scented gale;
While the flocks bounded foldwards along the vale,
And the soberer herds from the distant plain
Were wending towards home in their lengthened train.
   'Twas eve; but there was not the softened hue
Which the twilight oft o'er the landscape threw:

I felt not the breath of the evening breeze;
I saw not the wave of the forest trees;
I heard not the warbler's vesper song;—
They had sunk in silence their woods among.
　　But the landscape was wrapped in a thickening gloom,
Like a funeral pall for a night of doom;
For a storm frowned dark from the western sky,
And the gloom deepened more as the storm drew nigh.
I listened;—the music of eve was stilled;
But heavy the distant thunder pealed.
I looked;—I saw not the sun's bright beam,
But there was the lurid lightning's gleam:—
And they came in fury,—the lightning's flash,
And the wild wind's sweep, and the thunder's crash;
The fire stream poured on the fear-struck sight
A moment of day,—then a deeper night
Sank black on all, while the forest reeled
'Neath the rushing blast, and the thunder pealed
Through the echoing heaven;—in that dread hour
How puny the arm of a *mortal's* power!
—But they passed away; the thunder's crash,
And the wild wind's sweep, and the lightning's flash,
And the dark cloud's gloom;—they rolled afar;
While the moon's mild beam, and the twinkling star
Again shed their light o'er the peaceful scene,
And the storm was gone,—as it ne'er had been.
　　I looked again;—the morning beamed,
And the golden rays of the bright sun streamed:
A richer blue in the ether mild,
And a lovelier hue in the flow'ret smiled.
The landscape was vested with softer green,
And the dewdrops pure in their silvery sheen
Were sparkling around in the morning ray,

And night had melted in cloudless day.—
I thought of an hour when round my *soul*
I had heard heaven's *justice*-thunders roll;
When dark clouds gathering o'er my head
Were filling a guilty heart with dread;
When I feared each flash of the wrath divine,
And tremblingly watched each nearing sign
Of a righteous anger's rushing power
That was making a sin-struck spirit cower.

    But the storm swept by;—the lightning dread
Left all unscathed my guilty head,
And the dark cloud melted as it passed
In showers of blessing, while the blast
Sank to the whisper of mercy's voice,
That bade the trembling soul rejoice
In peace and pardon, light and love.—
I looked;—'twas a starlit heaven above!
And bright-eyed angels seemed to gaze
In smiling myriads through the rays;
To watch the sinner's heaving breast,
And mark how its terrors sank to rest.
And then the light of angel eyes
Melted away in the brightening skies,
As silent, soothing, gently stole
The sense of pardon on the soul,
For *now* 'twas God's own smile that beamed,
And the rays of His mercy around me streamed;
The SUN had risen! The night was o'er;—
The SUN had risen, *to set no more!*

A MORNING WISH FOR A FRIEND.

Darkness retires, and the brightening morn
Smiles as he heralds the day new born.
Mists roll away from the mountain's brow,
And his head wears a circlet of sunlight now.
Night's savage prowlers to caverns glide,
As seeking in darkness their deeds to hide;
While, mounting majestic his radiant throne,
With the glance of a monarch who reigns alone,
The sun looks forth from his palace of light,
And bids from his presence the gloom of night.
Glittering dewdrops reflect his ray,
Songsters carol on hillock and spray,
The woodlands wave to the breeze's breath,
The ripple plays light o'er the lake beneath,
The flocks from the fold towards the uplands bound,
And the echoing hills with their voices sound:
Nature unanimous joins to pay
A tribute of joy to the welcome day.

But there's a day of a brighter beam,
For its light from a brighter sun doth stream:
Sin and sorrow's dark clouds from its brightness fly
And the *soul* gains a prospect to worlds on high.
'Tis a day that dawns from the realms above,
'Tis illumined by beams of eternal love:
'Tis a day whose light is the smile of God,
Shedding heaven-born peace in the heart abroad.
The gloom of grief, and the mists of care
Melt away in its radiance, while black despair,

Far chased by the beams of its glory, flies,
And leaves to the soul heaven's cloudless skies.

Sister, may *this* bright day be thine!
Around thy soul may its sunbeams shine!
Be thy path in the light of its brightening rays,
And its gladdening glory on "all thy ways;"
Revealing from heaven thy title clear,
"To mansions" of endless glory there!

A NIGHT THOUGHT.

I HAVE seen the meteor's transient light,
As, a moment, it gilded the gloom of night;
I have watched the shower of starlets bright
    That bespangled its glittering way:
But though dazzling the flash of its brilliant beam,
It has passed away like a fading dream,
And a sadder and deeper gloom would seem
    To mourn for the meteor's ray.

I thought 'twas an emblem of pleasure's power
O'er the mind of man in its mirthful hour,
When the clouds of care o'er the soul that lower
    To its transient ray give room:
A moment, its beams round the spirit play;—
A moment, the dazzled spirit is gay;—
A moment!—the meteor has passed away,
And there follows a deeper gloom.

THE LITTLE SHELL AT COVE ROCK.

Delicate, fragile, tiny shell,
Thou hast a wondrous tale to tell.
I find thee here on the ocean strand;—
The billows have borne thee safe to land:
Yet those billows have proved the proud ship's grave,
And have mocked the power of man to save,
As its shattered fragments far and wide
Were strewn on the shore by the surging tide.
But thou art here, and all unharmed !
Say, how hast *thou* its fury charmed,
That its mighty waves on their foaming breast
Should bear *thee safe* to a place of rest?

The rock rears high his haughty form,
And challenges proud the ocean storm;
And he tosses the wild waves raging back,
As his challenge provokes their fierce attack.
But again, and *again*, and *again* they come;
And vainly the rock resists its doom:
The waves are mighty, and *know* their might:—
" *Never* have we been vanquished in *fight !*
We *kiss* the sands of the yielding shore,
We *rend* the rock in his pride of power:
Be it soon, be it late, thy fate is sealed;
Be it soon, be it late, *thou shalt surely yield.*"
—And it yields at last: with a headlong leap
It buries its shame in the foaming deep,
And the waves toss high their plumy spray,
As they dance triumphant around their prey.

And yet, little shell, I find thee here,
And nothing hath wrought thee harm or fear;
Though shattered rocks, and a wreck-strewn shore,
Give tokens dire of the ocean's power.
Tell me, tiny, beautiful thing!
Filmy and frail as the butterfly's wing;—
An *infant's* finger could crush thee to dust;—
What hast thou then wherein to trust?
And whence thy courage and power to brave
The surging might of the wild sea wave?
"I have not braved the ocean's might;
I reared no front with the waves to fight.
I yielded me meek to the billow's force,
As it swept me along in its onward course.
My *weakness* was strength in the tempest's hour,
And my *safety* I found in the ocean's power."

. . . . . .

And here, if he would, might *man* discern
A truth he is "slow of heart" to learn.
He rears his will 'gainst the will of heaven,—
And his proudest plans are to fragments riven.
Let him meekly yield to the sovereign sway
That even the sea's "proud waves" obey;
And though over life's ocean tempests roar,
And wrecks are strewn over "life's last shore,"
Borne like the shell on the billow's breast,
He shall land in a haven of endless rest.

1858.

A TRIBUTE OF SYMPATHY TO THE DEFENDERS OF GLEN LYNDEN.

Away! Away! Away!
There are patriot voices calling!
 Glen Lynden's band
 Holds the foe in hand,
Though its watch-worn sons are falling.

Away to the mountain glen!
Where the warwhoop wild is yelling,
 And the savage howls
 As he darkly scowls
On the white man's flame-wrapped dwelling.

There is life-blood reeking there!
Where our slaughtered friends are lying;
 Not boldly slain
 On the battle-plain,
But each by his hearth-stone dying.

Away! Away! Away!
To horse, to rifle springing,
 While the widow's sigh
 And the orphan's cry
In our ears,—in our *hearts* are ringing!

They were dwelling in peaceful vales,
Nor fear nor danger knowing;
 'Midst their flocks spread wide
 O'er the mountain side,
And milk and honey flowing.

The vine and the fig-tree's cheer;—
The cornfields waving gladness,
    The shearer's throng,
    And the reaper's song
Left cause nor room for sadness.

There was childhood's guileless glee,—
There was maiden beauty blooming;
    There was ripe old age,
    With its wisdom sage,
And its honour,—life perfuming.

And there were thankful hearts
For peace and plenty given;
    The voice of prayer
    Ascended there
And the song of praise to heaven.

And where are they *now?*—Ah! where?
There are homeless orphans weeping;
    The widow's wail
    Is on the gale,
The sire in his gore lies sleeping.

   .   .   .   .   .   .

And are there dastard souls,
Whose homes these homes were shielding,
    Who can coldly read
    While their brothers bleed,
Nor aid nor pity yielding?

Brand "COWARD" on his brow!
Write "TRAITOR" on his bearing,

Who views from afar
   Our "homestead" war,
And basely shrinks from sharing!

To your arms! To your arms! Away!
What! *cease* from the strife?—No, never!
   Till the neck of the foe,
   To earth bent low,
We have *conquered* a peace FOR EVER!

Rev. H. H. Dugmore.

1851.

THE COLOURS OF THE FIRST 24TH.

RESPECTFULLY DEDICATED TO THE SURVIVING OFFICERS
AND MEN OF THE REGIMENT.

" PRESERVE the *colours*, MELVILLE! *We* stand *here ;*
And—to the *end*." 'Twas thus that PULLEINE spoke,
On ISANDLANA's dark and fatal day;
Firm and resolved his mien, and calm his words,
Though death was nigh him, and he saw it :—
                            The camp stormed
By overwhelming myriads, and the yells
Of savage victors ringing in his ears
Demon-like, while they drowned the dying groans
Of hundreds, sinking low beneath the stroke
Of the blood-reeking Zulu assegai ;
O'erwhelmed, but *not* dishonoured.
                              They had fought
As British soldiers fight,—tens against thousands,—
Till the last charge was spent; and then,—"cold steel"

Grew hot in Zulu life-blood, and in heaps
Their dying foes lay round them.—'Twas in vain!
Hundreds had strewn the ground before their fire;
Yet, heedless of their fall, had *thousands* more
Recklessly trampled them in onward rush,
And wild contempt of death.
                           As the surf breaks
And strews with spray the shore, wave urging wave,
Blind to its leader's fate,—the Zulu host
Rolls its dark waves,—*its* dead, as yet, unmissed,
With thousands in reserve to fill their place.
   Man after man the British soldier falls,—
Falls where he stood,—his right arm's strength exhausted,
And his *dead* foes hurled on his bayonet's point,
To clear the way for others!
                           PULLEINE saw
His own end near,—and gave his dying charge:—
"Preserve the COLOURS! Let no savage hands
Stain the old honour of 'the 24th.'
Come *death*,—if come it must, but *not* disgrace!"
   And MELVILLE took the COLOUR,—*sacred trust!*
And bore it from the field. One farewell grasp,
One mutual gaze, and then they sadly part,
Comrades in arms, to meet on earth no more.
"Men of the 24th. *I* stay with *you;*—
We bide it to the end."—A ringing cheer
Shows the old fire unquenched; and though no hope
Of succour nerves their arm, they face the foe,
Till men and their commander sink together,
And join in death their comrades gone before.

     .   .   .   .   .   .

   The fight is done:—the cannon's boom is stilled;
Stilled is the rocket's rush,—the rifle's ring.

The yell of onslaught,—the defying cheer,—
Wails of the wounded, and the dying groan
Rise on the breeze no longer; nor the shrieks
Of hapless followers of the camp, unarmed,
And slaughtered in their helplessness.—The spoils
In savage triumph proudly borne away
With battle song of victory, upraised
By myriad voices 'mongst the echoing hills,
Are passing from the scene. The hush of death
Has settled all around; and gloomy night
Spreads her dark pall o'er the now silent field.
 But where is MELVILLE? How shall *he* escape?
Leagues must he traverse of a hostile land
Ere he can safely place his sacred trust.
And, scattered far and wide in headlong flight,
"Native Contingents" from the field of death
Urge their fear-stricken way with failing strength;
While ruthless foes, red-handed, strike them down
On every side. "Where? where is *he?* the guardian
Of his dead regiment's honour? Who shall say?
For, be it that he fights his way alone—
Horseman or footman, through the host of foes—
Or be it he evades their hot pursuit,
There crosses still his path, and bars his way,
The river boundary in summer flood,
The swirling waters as they rush and roar,
Mock at the wearied limbs that reach their banks,
And can *no more*, although the foe is on them !
Numbers die here; numbers plunge in—and drown.
Dies Melville too? Have any seen him fall?
Or has he dared the river with his charge?
Grasping the COLOUR, could he breast the flood?
Or is he swept away? Alas! none knows.

Explore the river ! search its wooded banks ;—
Men, horses, arms, caught 'midst entangling branches,
May yield *some* relic of the lost one,—
                                        Ah !
Who lies *here?* MELVILLE !—And who lies *here?*
COGHILL *with* MELVILLE, side by side in *death !*
Slain, though the raging flood was braved and conquered :
Slain, though escaped the hot pursuit beyond :
Slain in a mutual, last attempt to save
From the wild waters *that*—than LIFE more dear.
Hard, hard the fate—wrecked when the port was gained !
   Shield we from vulture's greed the sad remains,
By hasty cairn—and breathe a hurried prayer—
'Tis all we can—till worthier rites be paid—
But hark ! that shout ! "The COLOUR ! lo ! the COLOUR !"
Snatched from the turbid waters, drenched and torn,
But SAVED ! by friendly branches caught and held.
Hark how the glen resounds ! Cheer answers cheer ;
And the wild rocks with rapturous echoes ring.
   They are not " 24th " men who have found
The prize and its dead guardians :—What of that ?
They share a soldier's sympathies, and feel
The joy of brother soldiers as their own.
Mark now the swift return, while, borne aloft,
The sacred emblem challenges from far
The eager outlook—Ha ! 'tis seen ! 'tis seen !
The quick-eyed sentinel has caught it, and
There bursts the shout exultant from his lips.
The spark electric sets the camp on fire ;
"The COLOUR ! lo ! the COLOUR ! HONOUR SAVED !"
Rush from all sides the eager throng to greet
And welcome—while with cheers the camp resounds.

And now once more in martial order stands
The remnant of the regiment, to receive
And place in its old shrine the rescued treasure.
A guard of honour from the reverent hands
Of those who bear it take the precious pledge—
More precious for its perils—and it rests—
Dearer than ever in the regiment's heart.

MELVILLE and COGHILL! twins in death—your names
Belong to history! On Fame's bright scroll
They stand already blazoned. Men from far
Shall visit as a shrine your hero grave;
And grey-haired veterans in after years
Shall tell their children how, long, long ago,
At ISANDLANA's deadly, woe-fraught fight,
Ye saved the honour of "the 24th,"
And DIED IN SAVING IT!

Rev. H. H. Dugmore.

OUR BOYS.

"OUR boys came back from the army's van;
Toilworn with travel each horse and man,—
Bronzed nigh to blackness each face and hand,—
But bright every eye of the youthful band.

They had sprung "to the front" at the war's first call,
And a warrior's welcome had greeted them all.
"*First in the field!*—'twas your *father's* wont;
And the right to your place in the army's front,
Through the whole campaign ye shall yield to none,
Rest horses awhile, boys, and then,—march on;

Elliot and *Bailie* your leaders shall be,
And your post the heights of the deep Bashee."

. . . . . .

Loud through the camp the "Assembly" rings;
Quick to the saddle each horseman springs,—
And "Eastward ho!" is the warlike cry,
As "Headquarter" cheers give a warm "Good-bye!"

The camp is reached, the "Division" joined,
The "arms of the Service" all combined;
The "fellows" of "Number 6" are there,
Ready each peril and toil to share;
Second to none in the pluck they show,
And eager as any to face the foe.
There are black "allies," but with leaders *white*,
To show them the way the "English" fight.

And now they chafe at the long delay;
The halt grows tedious from day to day.
Weary of seeing the wild war-dance
They long for the welcome word "Advance!"
The foe is escaping, and drives afar
His flocks and herds from the field of war.

The slow-footed order comes at last,
And the camp wakes up at the trumpet's blast;
The column forms quick, as the bugles ring,
The skirmishers scatter on either wing
Where the war-song rises in savage pride,
And its echoes come back from the mountain side.

Few are the chances of open fight,
But enough to tell that the hearts are right, ·

And eager for battle with warriors bold,
While sparing and shielding the helpless and old.
Once and again is the issue tried,
Ere sinks the "sons of Kauta's" pride.
Once and again!—'tis useless all;—
They front the white man but to fall.

And now on the march, to wondering eyes,
The land's bright beauties around them rise;
The green hill's verdure,—the vale's soft sweep,—
The beetling crag on the mountain steep.
The view sublime o'er the gorges grand,
Where the Bashee winds towards ocean's strand.
While fountains sparkle—and woodlands wave
O'er the shore that the sea's blue waters lave.
Alas! alas!—with its beauties rare,
That the war-smoke should blacken a land so fair.

All is not sunshine; storm-winds rise,
And torrents pour from the darkened skies:
Dreary the march o'er the mist-clad heights,—
Weary the watch through the dark cold nights;
Baffling the beat of the driving rain,
Baulking the conflict again and again.
But no chilled spirits;—the hearts beat strong,
And the fiercer the rainstorm the louder the song.

"Our Boys" came back when their work was done;—
O'er river and mountain their march had gone,
They had stood on Umtata's farther shore,
Where no white man's army had stood before.
The foe is scattered,—the land is swept,
By the bands in the rear the "drifts" are kept.

But the toil is telling,—the steeds fail fast;
Umtata's battle must be the last.

Proud the dismissal "our Boys" receive:—
"First in the field, and the last to leave."
Prouder the welcome awaiting them here,
As the end of the homeward march draws near.
The cannon is booming!—"They come! They come!"
And the crowds thicken fast at the "Welcome Home!"
Where pennons are streaming, and banners wave,
To hail the return of the youthful brave.

Dark through the dust-cloud the column nears,
And hearts are throbbing 'midst rising tears.
Mothers and sisters, with straining eyes,
Are striving to pierce the strange disguise
In which toil, and combat, and dust, and storms
Have almost hidden the well-known forms
Of sons and brothers long lost from view,
And now emerging to life anew.

To the burst of "The conquering heroes come;"
To the tenderer strains of "Home, sweet home!"
Their march holds still through the thronging crowd,
While kerchiefs are waving, and cheers ring loud,
Till they halt at the spot where the march began,
When they started to join the army's van.

"Our Boys" had come back to rest awhile;—
To sun each heart in a mother's smile;—
To tell in a sister's or loved one's arms
The thoughts that had cheered them 'midst war's alarms.
And fathers were waiting with hearts that swell,
To learn if their "lads" had borne them *well*,—

And the warrior spirit had waked to life
In the *first strange* vision of mortal strife.
And little prattlers were waiting there
More eager than any to claim their share,
Looking with wondering hearts and eyes
On trophy shields and assegais,
And clustering round their knees to know
How their "big brothers" had beaten the foe.

Once more the "Assembly" rings aloud,
And the "Boys" muster fast 'midst the gathering crowd.
They have come their last "Dismiss!" to hear,
And bid good-bye to the camp's rough cheer,
To shake brave *Harvey's* warm right hand,
Who had headed them *well* through Galekaland.

. . . .

"Boys! I had thought to dissolve your ranks,
And send you home with your country's thanks.
But again from the mountains the war-cry sounds,
And the tribes on the border are breaking bounds;
The country may need you, hearts and hands,
While taming the pride of the Gaika bands:
Are you willing to answer a *second* call?"
"*Willing! aye Willing!* One and All!"

The response rang out, to be drowned among
The echoing cheers of the listening throng;
And if proud we had been of "our Boys" before,
Our triumph and pride gathered head the more,
As they turned from their homes to encamp again,
(With those homes in sight) on the tented plain.
Ready once more, at the trumpet's clang,
To spring to horse as at *first* they sprang.

Rev. H. H. Dugmore.

IN THE DROUGHT LANDS OF SOUTH AFRICA.

THE RAIN.

It was a land of rills,
Of mountains, kloofs, and hills;
High peaks were westward; eastward the great main—
A rich good land, and free
Men lived in liberty,
Worked and had quiet sleep, and loved the rain.

Thus was it for a time
In this fair sunny clime—
Flocks prospered; prospered, too, the bearded grain,
There only was good cheer,
And farmers felt no fear
When Nature's lavish bounties fell in rain.

But there came a change,
Clouds were few and strange—
The stored-up waters soon began to wane;
Broken and weak all day,
The streamlets ceased to play,
The sun glared on with no sweet veil of rain.

And lo! the land lay dry—
No moisture in the sky;
The streams dry—sterile the once fertile plain;
And round the empty tank
The ocean feebly sank—
Alas, why cometh not the wished-for rain!

The gentle animals whose fleeces give
The means whereby the people hope to live,
Lie down and die. It seems that ne'er again
Life-giving showers shall fall.
In churches now they call,
" O God, in mercy, send us down the rain ! "

All Nature cries aloud—
Oh, come, life-giving cloud !
The flowers, the grass, all herbage green is slain,
The corpse-like earth is black,
Skeletons form a track
O'er regions mourning for the want of rain.

Now has the joyful sight
Filled us with pure delight—
Of fatness dropping from the clouds again ;
From mountains to the sea,
One Hymn of Jubilee
Should thank the Master who has sent the rain.

Alex. Wilmot.

THE LANDING OF THE BRITISH SETTLERS OF 1820.

(*Written on occasion of the celebration of the Settlers' Jubilee in Grahamstown, in 1870.*)

WINDS of the North blew cold with icy breath,
And parting seemed a sorrow like to death,
When fifty years ago our little band
Of British settlers left their native land.

They said farewell for ever! ah, farewell
The friends, the joys, the land, they loved so well.
    We never more shall stand
    On that dear English land,
    Nor view our native skies;
    Gone each familiar face
    Of whose sweet loving grace
    Dear memories rise.

    Spring shall come back again,
    Smiling on hill and plain,
    We shall be gone;
    Our old homes will be gay
    With sunshine and the may,
    From our hearts flown.

    Farewell, dear land of birth!
    Farewell our native earth—
    Hill, plain, and river;
    Farewell, each dearest friend,
    May God all blessings send—
    Farewell for ever!

Away they go, 'midst mist and sudden gale,
O'er stormy seas, through Biscay's Bay they sail.
The sun is covered by dark lowering cloud,
And heaven seems hidden in a dusky shroud.
Hark! the huge vessel felt the thund'ring stroke,
While whelming waves in sudden deluge broke;
The seas around for horrid vengeance rave,
And every yawning gulf now seems a grave.

Again—the storm is o'er, with steady breeze
They glide in safety upon summer seas,

Whose azure surface as a mirror tries
To catch the sunny radiance of the skies.
Here gorgeous tinted sunsets come at even,
To show ten thousand gateways into Heaven—
While gentle zephyrs on the ocean play,
And balmy night succeeds the heat of day.

The twinkling beacons show how far they roam;
No longer the pale pole-star points our home;
The starry banners of the North are furled,—
The Southern Cross shines on a Southern world.
Now soon, with ecstasy, they hear the cry,
Land! land in sight! the land we can descry.
And now the longed-for shores before them rise,
With mountain peaks which fringe the azure skies;
Tall beetling crags frown o'er the breaker's roar,
Whose white-tipped billows kiss a sandy shore;
'Tis Afric! land of mystery and fear,
Of burning climate, and of desert drear,
Where the fierce lion and fiercer savage roam;
Here is your bourne,—here is your future home.

Supplies obtained within a western bay,
Again they sally forth upon their way,
And round that Cape which, hid in misty forms,
Towered o'er the ocean's verge "the Cape of Storms,"
Whose dangers Diaz did not fear to cope,
And proved it to the world Cape of Good Hope.
The oceans which this Cape for ever lave
While time shall last is that great sailor's grave;
And Nature's self proclaims his honours here,
By such a monument o'er such a bier.

Along the coast they sail. With pleasured eyes
They view new shores—new hills, new plains, arise,
The Cape St. Blaise and Longkloof Mountains past,
The hoped-for, longed-for haven comes at last;
Then, 'midst the glories of an April day,
They cast their anchor in Algoa Bay,
Whose outstretched arms receive in their embrace
Those dauntless settlers of a Northern race.
Here first brave Diaz stayed his vent'rous sail,
First here sought refuge from wild western gale,—
On a small isle, when tempests ceased to toss,
Planted Faith's emblem there, "The Holy Cross."
Religion's banner thus was first unfurled,
First reared within this savage Southern world.
Bare sand-hills line a tract of barren coast,—
No town, or village, can the seaport boast;
The vacant beach and bleak hill-side show clear
The work that waits the hardy pioneer:
O'er walls of surf they reach the welcome strand,
And the first British settlers touch the land.

   Upon this South-sea strand—
   Unto this savage land—
   Welcome, ye little band,
     Fit to brave danger.

   Losses and wars will be
   Fires of adversity,
   Tests which you cannot flee
     Trials and sorrow.

   Yours for success to fight;
   Yours to defend the right;
   Striving with all your might
     For life and freedom.

Under benignant skies,
Fruits on the plains shall rise,
As labour's sacrifice
    To the Creator.

Herds, flocks, and trade shall be
Proof of your industry,
Making prosperity
    Smile upon labour.

Sons of the great and free,
On! let your motto be,
"God and the right for me,
    Forward for ever."

Why come they here, amidst the desert's gloom?
To raise a nation from a lifeless tomb;
To bid fair plains the fruits of labour yield;
To tend the flock; to plough the fertile field;
The wealth of commerce by success to gain;
To found a home where peace and plenty reign.
These are your tasks: but oh! with hardships drear,
With toils unnumbered you must labour here;
For blasted crops, and floods, and drought shall come,
And savage yells around your burning home.
On toilsome sand they wander up and down,
Through numb'rous tents which form a canvas town;
With curious eyes all view the motley throng,—
Huge waggons dragging their slow length along,—
The wily Bushman and the Bechu'an,
The Hottentot, the Boer, and Englishman.
Here strange plants bloom beneath this southern sky,
And graceful aloes raise their blossoms high,

While prickly cacti and the feathery reed
Grow rank and common as the worthless weed.
And now they strike their tents. All "Parties" go,
They leave the sandy beach in waggons slow,
And cross the bushy plain, and Zwartkrops' stream,
Whose jungle-covered heights above them gleam;
O'er hills, o'er plains, they "trek"—and through the kloof,
Where the high rocky crags their paths o'er-roof,—
Where brilliant birds and gorgeous flowers are seen,
Screened by pavilions of perpetual green,—
Euphorbia raise their candelabra high,
And vivid bush o'er-curtains half the sky.

North, south, east, west, the settlers scatter wide,
By stream, by valley, and by mountain side.
They raise rough homesteads, and by labour's strain
Soon see around them fields of smiling grain.
Alas, their labour's vain! Too soon they view
The crops unhealthy, and of dusky hue;
Gaunt famine stalks upon the treach'rous soil,
And failures thrice renewed repay their toil.
Behold dark discontent with angry frown
Upon their hills and valleys settles down.
Again—dawn rises out of horrid night,
Relief has come and prospects are more bright;
They, now successful in the arts of peace,
Find, like the Argonauts, a golden fleece.

But trials still more hard have yet to come,
With Kafir yell and sight of blazing home.
The Kafirs long have angry passions nursed,
And now the flames from smouldering embers burst.

"Must we still retreat from the haunts of man
To the desert drear and the wild Bushman,
Where the lion and jackal are forced to flee,
With the wildebeeste and oribe?
Ah, no; in foray and vengesome fight,
We will dare the invader's utmost might;
And from bushy ambush again shall fly
Our shaft of destruction, the assegai."
The sky is lurid with a coming storm;
Against the white man common cause they form—
Their bands of hatred gather from afar,
And league together in a cruel war.
Fierce, treacherous, false, in untamed freedom bold,
The kloof or bush was still the Kafir's hold;
They sought not battle in the open field,
But used the weapons cunning loves to wield:
To lie in wait, to strike a sudden blow
Of ambushed vengeance on a dreaded foe;
With poisonous lies to sue for speedy peace;
To plot more murder in a brief release;
To pause, to strike with double force the blow;—
The flaming homesteads light them to their foe;
And women's screams for mercy, drowned in blood,
Cry out for vengeance to an angry God.
And foremost mingling in that awful strife,
The settlers fought for wife, for child, for life.
They see around them hideous signals rise,
The *Kafir's Fiery Cross* illumes the midnight skies.
They rush from burning homes, or die, as brave men die,
With face unto the foe and hopes in God on high.
And then, ye swarthy warriors, then began
Unequal warfare with the strong white man.

The assegai is measured with the gun;
The gage once taken up, war is not done
Till Hintza's death, and Gwanga's gory tide,
And Waterkloof, and many a red hillside,
And burning huts, and savage screams of woe,
Have proved the prowess of your British foe.
Three dreadful wars have Kafir fierceness proved,
And thrice their vengeance sought the white man's blood;
While thrice their warriors have been taught to know,
How vain their battle against such a foe.
Sir Harry Smith's and Cathcart's names rank high
With those renowned in English chivalry,
And many a nameless kloof's mimosas wave
O'er the brave British soldier's grave;
And Bowker's, Southey's, Currie's names shall be,
With those of others, kept in memory.*

Queenstown and Cradock's volunteers lay down
Their warlike weapons,—while King Williamstown
Rests on its arms by the Buffalo's side,
And starts new commerce on East London's tide.
The settler's city in success has grown,
And busy commerce smiles on Grahamstown;
And Port Elizabeth, their landing-place,
Still striding onward in progressive race,
Makes commerce speed its sails from Algoa Bay,
And sends new products o'er the watery way;

---

* Many brave colonists fought among the Burghers, and such names as those of White and Bailie (1835-6) will ever be remembered. Few survive of the early settlers who had to battle against the first difficulties and dangers. Such names as those of Godlonton, Chase, Wood, Cock, and Cawood occur to every one.

And far and near the bustling towns arise,
Planted and nursed by settlers' enterprise.
>   To God Almighty let us thanks upraise,
>   To Him all glory; to Him endless praise.

Now fifty years have passed.   Here is the field
Of dauntless energy, and this the yield;
Their advent here we celebrate in days
Which well can speak the British settler's praise,—
Their glory with their memory is blent,
THE EASTERN PROVINCE IS THEIR MONUMENT.

Alex. Wilmot.

IN THE COUNTRY OF MANKORAAN.

(NORTH OF THE VAAL RIVER, DECEMBER, 1882.)

> AH sad are our hearts,
>   Our souls full of trouble,
> Ruin's harvest has come—
>   We are left as the stubble.

> The white man is here
>   For our fields and our cattle;
> No hope is now left us—
>   No chance in the battle.

> We look on like men
>   Who are used to disaster,
> And see ruin's night
>   Falling faster and faster.

Or like animals struck
  By the swift assegai,
We are sentenced to death,
  We have only to die.

From Limpopo to Vaal
  Has the mandate been given,
" From his veld and his home
  Must the black man be driven."

From the homes of our youth,
  Which our eyes love to scan,
We are forced from the kraals
  Of our chief—Mankoraan.

We starve in the veld
  So blooming and verdant;
The invader is lord,
  The owner—his servant.

Christianity—lo !
  To your justice we fly;
Protect us at once,
  Or we perish and die.

Alex. Wilmot.

DRINK.

BEHOLD the Moloch of our Pagan days,
The Bacchic God, whom all his votaries praise;
For "Io Bacchus" is a modern hymn,
Chanted in praise of drink 'midst festive din.

The god is worshipped here in our own days,
Enshrined in radiance 'midst the hotels' blaze—
Or, where the drink-shop, with its beaming light,
Attracts the moth-like worshippers at night—
The sacrificial victims never fail,
With gait unsteady, and with features pale—
Still they come on; nor sex nor age is spared,
Recruits by thousands easily are snared;
Here comes the husband, with unsteady tread,
And offers up for drink his children's bread;
His weary wife soon learns to follow in,
And drown her wretchedness in draughts of gin;
The starving children, outcast and forlorn,
From Virtue's path at once are quickly torn.
Hence, from this nursery of sin and grief,
We get the outcast woman and cunning thief;
And the first lessons of the murderer's sin
Are taught in brawls amidst the tavern's din.
Moloch of drink! to thee are offered still
Youth, beauty, fortune, science, art, and skill;
Thousands of votaries drink thy poisoned cup,
And health, strength, life are freely offered up
In thy fell service. Life-blood still is poured
In new libations—neither plague nor sword
Obtains its victims, in the town or field,
In such abundance as thy altars yield.

" The cheerful cup, the drinking cup, goes round!'
Convivial spirits gladly hail the sound.
See here, in wretched misery, crawls along
The shadow of a man once hale and strong,
At one time wealthy—held in high esteem;
He loved, and was beloved—his upright mien

Told of an upright heart, till drink stepped in,
And all the train of curses following sin.
Then farewell heaven and friends, and peaceful life,
And welcome squalor, penury, and strife;
His once-loved partner learns from him to shrink,
Her life a martyrdom, her murderer Drink!
His son and daughter—God in heaven to be
The cause of such great crime and misery!
The girl, an outcast, walks the midnight street;
The boy skulks, trembling, 'fore policeman's feet.

" In festive houses festive cups go round!"
Widows and orphans shudder at the sound.
A death-knell tolls in every drinking song,
To some most heedless 'midst the drinking throng.
Ah! when the nations suffer, is it well
To wreath with flowers the portal of their hell?
When tens of thousands perish by the cup.
For neighbour's sake, for God's sake, give it up!
Its use is lawful, let its disuse be
Heaven's key for thee and thousands—Charity.

Not blasting fire from heaven so surely kills,
As burning draughts which flow from Bacchic rills.
See nations fall, as oaks by lightning stroke,
Their glories rivened, and their manhood broke.
Britain! "the Kafirs" curse before they die,
The cup—their poison, and thy infamy—
In Afric's land are riveted new chains,
And freedom flies when drunkenness remains.

Alex. Wilmot.

SOUTH AFRICA REDIVIVA.

BRIGHT land which stretchest down through Southern
    seas
On which the Sun loves well to look—South Africa—
Thou now hast wakened—and the stirring breeze
Which comes from the northward fills thee with a soul.
Arise, throw off thy shackles and advance—
Among the nations claim thy place, and live!
The time has come to shake off thy dull sleep
Of slavery and apathy: thou wast made to be
A home for millions of the brave and free.

For God has blest thee with a dower of wealth,
Of tree, of herb, of pasture, and of field:
Thy children laugh aloud in jocund health,
And all things men require thy plains can yield;
At faintest knock thy mountain portals ope,
Revealing treasure glimpses fair to see—
Rich diamonds, metals, aye, Imperial gold,
Are in the dower which God hath given thee.
Arise, ye Lotus-eaters of the South, and know
The plenteous blessings which from labour flow.

As men have reaped great Europe—pouring down
From Scandinavia and far Baltic's wave,
So must our future too be reaped—now sown,
The crops will grow above this era's grave.
South Afric calls aloud to Europe, filled
With overflowing energy and youth,
Come in your thousands—work as your fathers willed,

With strength, with power, with energy and truth.
Good Hope will turn to Hope at last fulfilled,
And Southern Africa be great—as God has willed.

Alex. Wilmot.

THE BEAUTIFUL ISLAND OF DREAMS.

> "They come, the shapes of joy and woe,
> The airy crowds of long ago,
> The dreams and fancies known of yore
> That have been and shall be no more;
> They change the cloisters of the night
> Into a garden of delight."—*Golden Legend.*

WHEN sorrow's dull clouds o'ershadow the soul,
   And the sunshine of life is concealed,
When the waves of misfortune still over us roll,
   There is sometimes a refuge and shield,
In a calm little harbour lit up by its sun,
   With genial though transient beams,
'Tis hailed as a shelter whene'er it is won—
   The Beautiful Island of Dreams.

When pursued by avenging demons of hate,
   The wretched oft pause in their path,
And find a retreat and a respite from fate—
   A brief lull in the tempest of wrath;
In the fair fairy bowers where in shadowy light,
   Illusion reality seems,
Whose oceans are bridged by the visions of night—
   The Beautiful Island of Dreams.

And still in this desert as onward we roam,
   On a dull and a desolate track,

Fast journeying on to Eternity's home,
  We sometimes in Dreamland look back;
And in slumber behold the dear friends that have gone;
  And the past or the future now seems
Rich with memory or hope to that oasis flown—
  The Beautiful Island of Dreams.

Alex Wilmot.

CAPE OF GOOD HOPE.

THERE is a land, unknown to fame,
A land whose heroes have no name
In the grey records of past age;
Unchronicled in hist'ry's page,
Untamed by art, yet wild and free,
That land lies in the Southern sea—
It laughs to heav'n which smiles on it;
There midway in wild waters set,
With suns serene and balmier breeze
Than ever swept these northern seas,
Its beetling crags rise vast, and war
With oceans, meeting from afar,
To break their billows on its shore,
With fearful never-ending roar.

Bold mariners who sailed of old
Through unknown seas in search of gold,
Saw those dark rocks, those giant forms,
And, fear-quelled, named them "Cape of Storms."
O land of storms, I pine to hear
That music which made others fear;

I long to see thy storm-fiend scowl,
I long to hear the fierce winds howl,
Hot with fell fires, across thy plains.

Thou glorious land! where Nature reigns
Supreme in awful loveliness,
O shall thy exiled son not bless
Those hills and dales of thine, where first
He roamed a careless child; where burst
Thy tropic splendour on his eye;
Where days were spent, whose mem'ries lie
Deep 'neath all afterthought and care,
Yet rise more buoyant than the air,
And float o'er all his days? O home
Of beauty rare, where I did roam
In childhood's golden days, my pray'r
For thee soars through this northern air.

Land of "Good Hope!" thy future lies
Bright 'fore my vision as thy skies!
O Africa! long lost in night,
Upon the horizon gleams the light
Of breaking dawn. Thy star of fame
Shall rise and brightly gleam; thy name
Shall blaze on hist'ry's later page;
Thy birth-time is the last great age;
Thy name has been, slave of the world;
But, when thy banner is unfurled,
Triumphant Liberty shall wave
That standard o'er foul slav'ry's grave,
And earth—decaying earth—shall see
Her freest, fairest child in thee!

William Rodger Thomson.

UTRECHT, 1856.

GOOD HOPE.

"Good Hope" for this good land yet,
    If we would but dare and do;
If we would but stand with ready hand
    To grasp ere the blessings go.

"Good Hope" for this good land yet,
    If we would but stay life-streams,
Which will past us flow while we, too slow,
    Stand rapt on the bank in dreams.

"Good Hope" for this good land yet,
    If we would but cease to hope
That the rain will drop and bring a crop
    While we idly sit and mope.

"Good Hope" for this good land yet,
    If we work, e'en while we wait
For the sun and rain to ripen grain
    We have sown, then left to fate.

"Good Hope" for this good land yet,
    If we use each heav'n-sent gift
As means to an end, and do not spend
    Our best without care and thrift.

"Good Hope" for this good land yet,
    If we live and struggle still
To a better life, through toil and strife,
    With a stout heart and strong will.

"Good Hope" for this good land yet,
  If our faith be active trust,
And not blind belief, which, at each grief,
  Still mourns that what must be, must.

"Good Hope" for this good land yet,
  If we would but trust in God,
And the Christ, who came and took our name
  To bless, not to turn the sod.

William Rodger Thomson.

ODE.

(FROM HORACE.—*Lib*. ii. *Od.* 18.)

No ivory—no golden ceiling
  Adorns my modest home;
No marble pillars, wealth revealing
  Proudly support the dome.
No regal fortune, princely dwelling,
  Hath fate vouchsafed to me,
I am not clad, in state excelling,
  In robe of sovereignty:
A vein of wit, by nature's blessing,
  And honest heart are mine.
· Yet me to honour, nought possessing
  The wealthiest incline ; .
Why should I then the gods importune
  To add unto my store,
Contented with my humble fortune
  I could not wish for more.

Day hastes to follow day, and truly
    New moons but come to die,
The tomb awaits thy ashes duly
    Mid all thy pageantry.
Yet mindless of the fatal hour
    On high thou build'st the hall,
Insatiate with thy wealth and power
    Thou fain would'st seize on all;
Thy neighbour's farm, thy neighbour's dwelling,
    All would'st thou have for thee,
'Gainst justice and 'gainst law rebelling
    With base cupidity;
While from their home unjustly driven
    The husband and the wife
(The babes exposed to winds of heaven)
    Must linger out their life:
But one sure homestead there remaineth
    Than all on earth more sure,
The dark abode where Orcus reigneth
    Alike o'er rich and poor,
Just earth entombeth ev'n the poorest
    With sons of royalty,
And Charon thou in vain allurest
    For gold to set it free:
Great kings renowned in ancient story
    He holdeth in his might,
Far famed of old for warlike glory
    Now doomed to endless night:
Invoked in pity he hath risen,
    And uninvoked,—to free
The hapless poor from their earth-prison
    And grant them liberty.

E. B. Watermeyer.

AFTER A STORM.

Morning has come upon us,—from the day
   Has rolled each darkling cloud, the orient view
   Unveils with gorgeous sun, and deep clear blue.
But ocean riots still ;—in ponderous play
Thousands of heavy surges plunge away,
   Dazzling with snow-white foam, or swiftly woos
   Iris to paint all brightly tinted hues.
Strangely fair magic, mid their shivered spray,
Around us many a little whale-bird skims,
Dipping its tiny bosom in the deep,
Then instantly uprises blithe and high,
Even as the heart unthralled by earthly things
Will walk this troubled earth yet ever keep
Its dearest home up in the azure sky.

                           E. B. Watermeyer.

AMMAP AND GRIET.

A LEGEND OF THE 'NOSOP.

On a huge rock of granite stone,
A dark-skinned maiden stands alone,
   Her eyes with vengeance gleam.
'Twas in a wild and savage glen,
Far from the busy haunts of men,
   Where 'Nosop rolls its stream.

And who is she? What does she there?
Alone beside by the lion's lair!
   Has she no woman's fear?
She had—but all that fear is gone,
She stands upon that very stone,
   Because she knows he's near.

"Dark-skinned maiden, come away,
Tempt not thus the beast of prey,
   Haste, haste, your life to save."
"No, no," the dark-skinned maiden cried,
"He tore my Ammap from my side,
   And vengeance I will have!"

A white man stood behind a tree,
A double-barrelled gun had he,
   And steady was his aim;
She knew not that his help was nigh,
But lightly poised the assegai,
   When forth the lion came.

He sees her! With a single bound
He strove to reach the vantage ground,
   But ere the rock he gained,
The dark-skinned maiden's aim was true,
Downwards the fearful weapon flew,
   And in his side remained!

He fell, and writhing in his pain,
Madly he strove, but strove in vain,
   To rise upon his feet.

"Ah, ah," the dark-skinned maiden cried,
"This day I was to be his bride,
He tore my Ammap from my side,
   Ah, ah, revenge is sweet."

Beneath that rock of granite stone,
On which the white man stands alone,
   The lion writhes in pain.
The dark-skinned maid is at his side
She drew a dirk, her Ammap's pride,
   He never rose again.

Some months had rolled away, and then,
Within that very lion's den,
   Were found the bones of Griet;
And to this day, who ventures nigh
That granite rock, will hear the cry,
   "Ah, ah, revenge is sweet!"

But visitors are very rare,
The native seldom ventures there,
   He rather turns aside.
And why? Because he fears to meet
The wandering ghost of faithful Griet
   With Ammap at her side.

                        S. A. M.

SONNETS OF THE CAPE.

I.

GOVERNMENT GARDENS, CAPE TOWN.

Oft, when my feet at evening homeward tread
   The stately cloisters of the oaks along,
   My fervent soul breaks into grateful song,
And I a glad, rapt worshipper am led.
God, what a glorious prospect is outspread!
   Impersoned nature here hath built her shrine:
   On yon great altar sacrifice divine
She offers to her Maker. On the head
Of the majestic peak upon the west,
   Her favoured seat, at eve oft sitteth she,
Soothing the busy city into rest,
   Whilst the sun setting lights the golden sea.
Here, in thy fane, bright Presence, I divest
   My heart of lower thoughts, and bow to heaven and thee.

II.

NIGHT.

Dost thou not love, O angel of the night,
   Above all others this fair southern land?
   For thou hast gemmed its skies with lavish hand,
With rarest stars and constellations bright.
Shines not its vestal moon with purer light?
   Hath not its galaxy more lustrous hue
   While star-clouds, set in heavens more deeply blue,
Still gladden ours, as erst Magellan's sight?

O would that while the old grey mountains sleep
   There might be silence in the which to find
Grand music! But if joyous creatures keep
   Perpetual chorus, shall my captious mind
Object? Creation's harmonies lie deep,
   But to the soul attuned the parts are well combined.

G. Longmore.

THE FADED PHOTOGRAPH.

TO MY FRIEND, DAVID C———, BATH, SOMERSETSHIRE.

Your portrait hangs upon my wall,
   Among my treasures highly classed,
For it is potent to recall
   Old days that we have passed
In close communion, heart and mind,
   Where Avon's placid waters wind.

And very often, as I gaze,
   Bath's noble hills with you I climb,
Or tread the valley's wooded ways
   Where we've roved many a time:
Delightful scenes that I would fain,
   Before I sleep, behold again.

Our Cape its beauties hath, 'tis true:
   Old Table Mountain's always grand,
Our sun is bright, our sky is blue;
   The Maker's bounteous hand,
From which all beauty hath its birth,
   Made this far corner of His earth.

THE FADED PHOTOGRAPH.

Yet must a Briton love his home
   The more for absence, as I ween,
And greatly do I long to roam
   Through daisied meadows green,
Perchance made dulcet by the swell
   Of distant chiming village bell.

O for a field of new mown hay,
   A beach, or elm, or tasselled birch;
A springtide scent of virgin May,
   Or a glimpse of an ivied church!
To tramp the stubbles of the corn
Upon a fresh September morn;

To tread once more with gladsome feet
   The thronging street, the busy mart;
To feel again the mighty beat
   Of England's wondrous heart!
But, though I long, I murmur not,
For Heaven appoints each human lot.

You know not how we exiles prize
   This modern photographic art,
Portraying to our grateful eyes,
   Exact in every part,
Kindred and friends forever dear;
We gaze, and almost think you here.

Your picture's somewhat faded now,
   But to fond memory it shows
Your very self; oft mark I how
   You wear your homely clothes.

You know what one professor teaches,
And I have faith in what he preaches.*

And oft I sit by your fireside,
   And share your daily household life;
Upon my knees the youngsters ride,
   Or I chat with your blue-eyed wife.
Give them my love, and tell them, pray,
Not to forget me far away.

Let time and age do all they can,
   And let it fade, if fade it will,
This portrait of a sterling man
   Shall grace my chamber still;
And I its dimmest lines shall trace,
Until I meet him face to face.

G. Longmore.

CAPE TOWN, *February* 1862.

EVELEEN.

My own girl at home,
   Weep no longer for me,
The ship steps through the ocean foam
   That bears me back to thee.
Full sail and bending mast,
   We cleave the waters green;
I'm hasting home to thee, at last,
   My own Eveleen.

---

* See "Sartor Resartus" *passim.*

EVELEEN.

I have o'ercome the fate
   That parted us so long;
I have o'erpast the treacherous hate,
   Forgot the rankling wrong.
I am speeding o'er the sea
   They swore should roll between
The one who loves thee well, and thee,
   My own Eveleen!

Of you, how many a night
   I've dreamed, the long watch through!
From noon's brain-searing shafts of light
   My thoughts have flown to you.
To you in your own home bowers,
   Where the light falls cool and green,
My saint of saints! my flower of flowers!
   My own Eveleen!

But now no longer pine,
   No longer wait and weep;
Our pennant floats far o'er the brine,
   We march along the deep.
With store of royal gold,
   With silks of sunny sheen,
And bridal raiment meet to fold
   My own Eveleen.

An hour! and he shall trace
   The old home seen once more;
But to have seen his true love's face
   White as the shroud she wore!

Oh, fading human love!
  Oh, light in darkness seen!
Oh, voiceless as the stone above
  Thy grave, Eveleen!

C. P. M.

MOZAMBIQUE CHANNEL,
  November 1861.

FAREWELL TO MADEIRA.

HARK! hear the billow swell;
Bright Madeira, fare thee well,
Shining mountains, azure skies,
Sunniest hearts and friendliest eyes:
All my soul has felt so long,
Like a joyous flow of song,
Sinks at vesper's distant bell,
Loved Madeira, fare thee well.

Summer island, now no more
Shall I move along thy shore,
Where in all thy waves I caught
Oracles of peaceful thought;
Mid thy glittering walls and towers,
Girt by vines and gay with flowers,
Oft in sleep shall fancy dwell:
Loved Madeira, fare thee well.

Rock-built isle, whose mountains rude,
Are the throne of solitude;
Where from giant crag and steep
I have gazed on valleys deep,

Feeling powers within me pass
From each stern aerial mass;
Land of lovely peak and dell,
Loved Madeira, fare thee well.

Far within the cares of life,
Hushed beyond the sound of strife,
Where, methinks, thy spirits call
From thy soothing waterfall;
Oft shalt thy remembrance be
Quiet strength and joy to me,
Brightening mem'ry's dusky cell,
Loved Madeira, fare thee well.

From the heights of time and toil,
Where I stand on heavenly soil,
Far around, discerning clear
Many a various land and year,
Most the vision seems to smile
Warmed by the Hesperian isle;
Round thee floats a sunny spell,
While I murmur, fare thee well.

Often magic lures me far
Toward the East's familiar star;
Older powers with earlier sway,
Chanting call me hence away;
And I hear above thy foam,
Trembling round the voice of home,
Whispering more than tongue can tell—
Yet, Madeira, fare thee well.

On thee still may summer breathe,
Still thy crown with blossoms wreathe;
And may still, with peace divine,
More of noblest life be thine:
Making hearts of kindliest mould
Earnest, glad, serene, and bold.
So, supreme all ill to quell,
God, fair island, keep thee well!

John Stirling.

FAREWELL TO FIFTY-FIVE.

Farewell, farewell, old Fifty-five! to thee,
This circling ball no longer homage yields;
  Thy record's closed, and frail humanity
Stands trembling 'neath the rod that conscience wields.
  For now, methinks, that record's page reveals
A long dark roll of follies, faults, and crimes
  Before His eye, whose love in vain appeals
To hearts ingrate; whose goodness glads our times,
  And spreads with genial gifts the wide earth's varied climes.

Upon thy wingèd hours, old Fifty-five,
Alternate hopes and fears have trembling hung,
  Capricious as the fleecy clouds which drive
Athwart the summer sky, a motley throng
  Of joys and griefs, have swiftly swept along.
Now o'er the welkin peal the bridal bells;
  Anon the mournful funeral dirge is sung;
Big with this truth each passing moment swells,—
  "Beyond the sky alone unchanging pleasure dwells."

Farewell, old Fifty-five! the visions fair
Which down thy sparkling vista erst appeared,
  Beguiling Mammon's votaries with the glare
Of sordid wealth in pile on pile upreared,
  Have flitted past, and left a blank, uncheered
By one bright gleam, in many an aching breast.
  O were the sober truth more wide revered,
And gaping folly's golden dreams repressed,
    How few would groan beneath the gambler's dark unrest.

Few were our tears, old Fifty-five, hadst thou
Consigned alone the noisome vampire band
  To disappointment blank, and carking woe :
But thou with undiscriminating hand
  Hast flung on poverty's inclement strand
Full many a one styled "noblest work of God."
  His lowing herds have perished from the land,
Or haply o'er his fields a blight has trod ;
    Still, *he* can trusting say, "My Father holds the rod."

Farewell, old Fifty-five ! bright o'er thy days,
Celestial truth has flung her radiant bow ;
  Benignant from her throne she stoops to raise
Each moiling slave of ignorance and woe.
  Her silv'ry voice proclaims to high and low
This blood-bought truth, "man's mind and tongue are free."
  May every human breast responsive glow,
Till superstition, pride, and bigotry,
    Their lofty heads abase, and like grim spectres flee.

Farewell, old Fifty-five! inhuman war
With blood-red hand has o'er thy cycle swept.
  Horrific still he rolls his thund'ring car
'Mid ghastly wounds, and dying groans unwept.
  The cannon's roar which long in silence slept,
Unceasing echoes o'er the dismal scene;
  Deep blushing, Mercy from her throne has stept,
While eager Rapine stalks with hideous mien,
  And gloating scan's the flaming city's lurid sheen.

  O Liberty! Britannia's proudest boast;
O Liberty! man's brightest heritage;
  Why on thy steps attendant should a host
Of sanguinary passions fiercely rage?
  Or why should history's memorable page
Be blotted o'er with sighs and groans and tears?
  When will grey time mature the golden age,
When men shall snap their swords and quiv'ring spears,
  And Peace triumphant reign o'er all the circling years?

  Farewell, old Fifty-five—as ling'ring still
Thy last faint echoes on the ear expire,
  And sadd'ning thoughts the heaving bosom fill,
Hope strings anew her animating lyre.
  Eternal truth—the soul's immortal fire—
Ere long shall claim the homage of the world,
  High o'er gaunt Slavery's blazing funeral pyre
Shall Freedom's crimson banner wave unfurled,
  And Ignorance and Vice from their dark thrones be hurled.

William Selwyn.

PORT ELIZABETH, *January* 1, 1856.

"LEAD, KINDLY LIGHT."

"A little earthen lamp, 1700 years old, was recently found in the East, which bore this inscription—'The light of Christ shines for all.'"
—*Christian Express*, December 1, 1878.

This tiny lamp of fragile clay
Once shed its faint and flick'ring ray,
   To cheer perchance some sage's hall;
Its light extinct, 'mid wreck it lies,
Through seventeen rolling centuries;
Till disentombed, behold the truth,
Bright with the glow of pristine youth,
   "The light of Christ shines for us all!"

Hail, glorious truth! Thy music thrills
In echoes from time's distant hills;
   And still thy tones melodious fall.
Still may poor wand'rers lift their heads
To Him, whose face benignant sheds
Effulgent rays, to warm and cheer,
To waken hope, and banish fear;
   "The light of Christ still shines for all!"

The ice-built screens by bigots planned,—
As children's barriers in the sand,
   Dashed by the wild waves, sink and fall—
Melt in the beams from Jesus' face,
Exhale in mist and leave no trace:
Free as the breeze on mountain side,
Wide as the ocean's rolling tide,
   "The light of Christ still shines for all!"

Light, light for Afric's dusky throng;
Light for the pris'ners held so long
   In superstition's blinding thrall;
Light for the savage and the sage,
For smiling youth, and trembling age;
Light for all sorrowing, sin-struck eyes
That seek the pathway to the skies;
   "The light of Christ still shines for all!"

W. Selwyn.

PORT ELIZABETH, *December* 11, 1878.

"SHOULD IT BE ACCORDING TO THY MIND."

(JOB xxxiv. 33.)

SHALL feeble, vain, presumptuous man
Whose loftiest vision's but a span,
Impugn the vast mysterious plan
   By boundless wisdom laid?
Shall His omnipotent behest,
That thunders o'er wild ocean's breast,
Or lulls its surging waves to rest,
   By puny worms be stayed?

Shall man, whose moments hurrying flee,
Like sparklets from a phosphor sea,
Prescribe to dread Eternity
   The laws of His domain?
Shall He who scans each circling pole,
And points the course the planets roll,
Seek wisdom from the darkling mole
   To guide the shining train?

Shall yon vast orb whose kindling ray
Pours forth the universal day
His glad, majestic progress stay,
   Lest, haply, his bright beams
With light unwelcome should illume
The drowsy couch, and chide the gloom
Of some voluptuous sluggard's room,
   And chase his idle dreams?

Shall thirsty nature pant in vain
For showers of life-restoring rain;
Shall desolation sweep the plain
   And beauty droop and die;
Lest one bright drop's exultant spring
Should snap the spider's airy string,
Or dim, perchance, the golden wing
   Of some gay butterfly?

Shall yon glad stream, whose sparkling tide
Spreads verdant beauty far and wide,
O'erleap its banks and turn aside,
   Or in the desert sink;
Lest, haply, fraught with summer showers,
Its waves should ripple o'er the flowers
By children planted 'mid the bowers
   That tangle on its brink?

No! He, whose power with life endued
This glorious universe, pursued
In His design the highest good
   And happiness of all;

And still, at His benign command,
Rich bounties gladden ev'ry land,
And still He guides, with all-wise hand
    Each tenant of this ball.

O! then, low-bending in the dust,
Cling to His LOVE, with child-like trust,
Believing that Omniscience must
    Know what for thee is best;
Let resignation soothe thy cares;
Let faith disperse thy gloomy fears;
And God Himself shall dry thy tears
    In His eternal rest.

W. Selwyn.

PORT ELIZABETH, *January* 21, 1879.

TO GRAAFF REINET.

HAIL! "Gem of the Desert," in slumber reposing,
    The dark hills thy cradle, soft verdure thy bed;
The breeze from the kloof richest perfumes disclosing,
    Lightly sweeps o'er thy bosom, raising dust very red.

The last gleams of the sun in gay splendour descending
    Seem fondly to linger around the tall spire,
While the clouds, rainbow-tinted, their gorgeous hues lending,
    Make the Dutchmen's black chimneys seem as if all afire.

Deep bosomed in shade the dark river meanders,
  Save where, like a mirror, it gleams from the glade;
Or soapy and slimy through mud-holes it wanders,
  Where stockings are washed by a Hottentot maid.

Sweet abode of content; dearly loved Graaff Reinet!
  Long, long mayst thou bask in thy slumber profound;
Tame spring-bucks be baited for a sixpenny bet,
  And thy butter be sold at four shillings per pound.

W. Selwyn.

GRAAFF REINET, 1860.

HYMN.

WRITTEN DURING THE ZULU WAR.

"And I, if I be lifted up from the earth, will draw all men unto me." |
—JOHN xii. 32.

O SAVIOUR throned in peace above
  Reveal Thy piercèd side,
And let the vision of Thy love
  Stay war's remorseless tide;
    Risen Saviour, hear!

For white, for black, alike didst Thou
  Low bow Thy fainting head;
For all of ev'ry clime and hue,
  Didst Thou thy heart's blood shed.
    Suffering Saviour, hear!

Behold fair Afric's sunny lands
  With reeking carnage strewed,
See God-made man with rigid hands
  In brother's blood imbrued;
    Sorrowing Saviour, hear!

O hear the Briton's dying groan,
  The Zulu's piercing wail;
O hear the famished orphan's moan,
  The widow's sobbing tale;
    Pitying Saviour, hear!

In mercy stay the quiv'ring spear;
  Avert the death-winged ball;
Pour balm for ev'ry scalding tear,
  And breathe Thy peace o'er all.
    Mighty Saviour, hear!

Draw weary warriors round Thy feet
  By love's constraining cord;
There let the scattered nations meet,
  And hail Thee Sov'reign Lord.
    Gracious Saviour, hear!

William Selwyn.

PORT ELIZABETH, *February* 9, 1879.

THE LAMENT

OF THE GUTTER LATELY FILLED UP BY AN UNPOETICAL MUNICIPALITY.

Old residents of Port Elizabeth will remember the kloof running down between Donkin Street and Constitution Hill, which was spanned by a rude wooden foot-bridge just opposite Dr. Edwards' residence. The kloof having been filled up now forms the site of the row of houses on the right-hand side of Donkin Street. This municipal improvement forms the subject of the following pitiful "Lament." Whatever may be thought of the merit of the verses, the author takes some credit for an eye to the "practical," for the attempt to lead off the surface water through an underground culvert, resulted in the catastrophe predicted in the concluding verses within a very short time after the completion of the work.

OH list, good folks, a tale of woe,
    A tale of dark oppression,
Let briny tears your cheeks down flow
    In sorrowful procession.

Till late I trickled down the glen,
    In sunbeams gaily sparkling;
But now, entombed by heartless men,
    I creep on cold and darkling.

Beneath a huge chaotic mass
    Of rubbish vile I mutter;
Mid frogs and fungi rank, alas!
    A melancholy gutter.

No more my channel, decked with green,
    Relieves the eye aweary.
Its verdant slopes no more are seen,
    But all around is dreary.

THE LAMENT.

No more the breeze, with fitful sigh,
    Along my bed breathes mildly,
No more, when Boreas blusters high,
    My caverns echo wildly.

The rustic bridge, that bound my banks
    In brotherhood together,
Is torn away, and its rude planks
    Are gone—"the Board" knows whither.

Away! a dire revenge I'll brew;
    My rage, meanwhile, I'll bung tight.
That sordid "Board" the day shall rue
    When next I see the sunlight.

When turbid torrents rushing pass
    Adown my peeping square holes,
Right through this execrable mass,
    I, madman like, will tear holes.

I'll heave aloft the lumb'ring load,
    And crashing down I'll toss it,
Till in the middle of the road *
    I make a "fixed deposit."

William Selwyn.

---

* Query, on the "Banks"?—*P. D.*

MY "SALTED" STEED.

Oh! give me back my "salted" steed,
   They said, he would not die,
They said of stable I'd no need,
   But told a dreadful lie.
I let him out one moonlight night—
   Upon the grass he fed—
And in the morning, cruel sight!
   My salted steed was DEAD.

I bought him with a good "Bewijs,"
   And thought to get my geld—
So wrote a letter in a trice,
   And sent it through the veld;
But when the man who sold him came
   And opened his inside—
He said the "paapjes" were to blame,
   And that was how he died!

I've had a dozen steeds or more,
   Since that eventful day;
But no more "salted" ones, be sure—
   That sort of thing don't pay,
For if a charger's worth a sou,
   He's worth his feed, I swear:
And should he live, I laugh, don't you?
   And should he die, don't care.

A. Brodrick.

TRANSVAAL.

A ROMANCE FROM THE FIELDS.

A COLONIAL BALLAD.

"How be I getting along, sir?
   Why, thankee, I can't complain;
The taties and crops looks splendid,
   Since we got that there last rain:
The cattle and birds does middling,
   The missus and children's well,
And the future looks bright and cheery,
   So far as I can tell.

"I look like a Dutchman, do I?
   With them feathers in my hat!
Well p'r'aps they're a trifle gaudy,
   But I'll wear 'em 'spite of that.
My 'talisman' I calls 'em, for
   They came off a wondrous bird,
That completely changed our fortunes:
   'Tis the strangest tale you've heard.

"Afore you left for England,
   You may mind I went to the Fields;
I was nigh played out with farming,
   And read of the thumping yields
Them diamond claims was giving, so
   Resolved my luck to try,—
The drought and cruel lungsick
   Had bothered us proper*ly*.

"I got what I could together,
  And we started right ahead;
Missus and me and Bill here,
  With two little gals as is dead.
I didn't do much at digging,
  But money could then be earned
By any willing fellow
  Who to work in earnest turned.

"Wages was high, and I prospered,
  Till fever came to the place,
And I was unable to work, sir,
  And our children drooped apace.
'Twas a sad time, I can tell you,
  And oft should we have starved,
But a neighbour—he'd been a sailor—
  His substance with us halved.

"Good? I should say that he *was* good,
  A thorough kind-hearted brick—
Poor fellow! before very long though,
  He himself fell sorely sick.
My wife did all she could, kind soul,
  And nursed him night and day;
But with me and the children poorly,
  She'd a hardish part to play.

"Poor Jim didn't get no better,
  And it seems made up his mind,
As how he must die at the Fields, sir,
  And all he'd to leave behind

Would 'queath to my missus, who always
    Had been his kindest friend—
'Twasn't *much*, for things were dear then,
    And his coin had come to an end.

"Well! all there was he made over,
    Then poor Jim was laid to rest—
We got his watch and knicknacks,
    But what the wife liked best
Was a couple of Dorking hens, sir,
    And a fine young Spanish cock;
Quite right, sir, them's the feathers,
    That I fear give you a shock.

"The missus was fond of poultry,
    And was pleased with what we'd got;
But hunger is hard to bear, sir,
    So the birds came to the pot.
Our little gals lay a dying,
    And food we all must have,
So one by one the fowls were killed,
    But our bairns we could not save.

"The young cock's turn came last, but
    To kill him we all were loth;
But Billy and me in the fever lay,
    So the wife made us some broth.
And now was the strangest thing, for when
    That bird was drawn, his crop
Contained—well, guess?—I assure you,
    My wife was fit to drop.

"A diamond? Yes! a brilliant,
    Without a fault or flaw,
As good a gem, for its size, you know,
    As ever merchant saw.
Four hundred pounds we sold it for,
    And we bought shares in a claim
That doubled soon the sum we had:
    Don't that *bird* deserve some fame?

"Thank God, the fever left us,
    Little Billy was first to mend;
And after a while I got stronger,
    And could to work attend.
But we'd all had enough of the Fields, sir,
    And longed to come back home;
To settle down in the dear old place,
    Nor want again to roam.

"I look like a Dutchman, do I?
    Well! all that we have we owe
To that young bird, I reckon;
    And my gratitude I shall show.
I shall sport his blue-black plumes then,
    For it does not oft betide,
When killing a fowl to cook, you find
    A *plum* in his inside."

C. F. *Overton.*

THE FLIGHT OF THE AMAKOSA.

A RIFLE CORPS LEGEND.

It's the hour of the morn
When he who's not born
With a silver spoon ready-made for him, will scorn
 To muddle his head
 By lying in bed,
But jumps into a tub of cold water instead;
 Which disperses each dream,
 And gets up his steam,
And makes him as fresh as new butter and cream;
 Drives off sleep's dizziness,
 Fits him for business,
 Screws up his system,
 And seems to assist him
To follow whatever employments enlist him.

In short, it's the hour when the whole *Ville du Cap*
(As the Frenchmen call Cape Town) wakes up from its nap
And prepares for its trade, its profession or craft, as
Labourer, lawyer, or dealer in baftas.

 But every one knows
 That although *l'homme propose*,
It isn't in mortals themselves to "dispose,"
For that is undoubtedly *toute autre chose*—
Or to speak in plain English, when plain English suits—
A pair of decidedly different boots.

THE FLIGHT OF THE AMAKOSA.

      And so on this day
      Quite a different way
Of spending its time—neither work nor yet play—
      From what Cape Town chalked out
      When first it had walked out
That morning, it found in its destiny lay.
For Brown, Jones, and Robinson, Thomson, Smith, Russel,
And Jack, Tom, and Harry, are all in a bustle,
      Crying, "Holloa! what now?
      What's the news? what's the row?
      What the deuce can the matter be?
      What can the clatter be?"
Kafirs escaped from the Amsterdam Battery!

      It's really true:
      And one looks blue
And another knows hardly what to do:
      Some stare, and some
      Look shockingly glum,
While others declare it's "remarkably rum."
      "Why don't they bring Inspector King,
And his blue-coat 'peelers?'—that's the thing?"
      While others shout,
      "What are they about?
Why don't they call the artillery out?"
      But voices are drowned
      By a martial sound
That all on a sudden rings out around;
      And each who hears
      Cries out, "Three cheers!
It's the bugle-call of the Volunteers!"

Over the chimney-pots, over the tiles,
Over the gardens, two square miles,
Float the sounds of that warlike blast,
Proclaiming approaching relief at last.
  Doubt has fled,
   Fear hides its head,
And curiosity reigns instead.

  . . . . . .

In the square of the Church there's a hubbub and fluster,
In the square of the Church the brave warriors muster—
Cavalry warriors armed, spurred, and booted,
With white-covered caps for the atmosphere suited,
Jackets of blue, rather short in the waist,
Garnished with silver in beautiful taste,
Trousers of blue with a broad silver border
And very long swords of the steel-scabbard order.
  One by one,
   To see the fun
The citizens into the Church square run,
  And then they gaze
   In delighted amaze
At the gallant scene the square displays,
As the warriors gather by twos and threes
Beneath the shadow of two small trees,
Twirling mustachios in solemn monotony—
Excepting the captain, who hasn't yet got any,
  · While a few little boys
   Are making a noise
   And shouting, "Oh my!
   Here comes a guy!
Oh come and look at this rummy fella
A riding up with his umberella!"

   And truth to confess,
   It *did* look a mess,
As a hero rode up on his gallant Black Bess,
   And while he wore
   His costume *du corps*,
In his hand a white-covered umbrella he bore.

   The muster's complete,
   Each man's in his seat,
Ready to do any desperate feat.
   The captain springs
   To his saddle, and flings
A look which alone attention brings;
   Ere he gives the word,
   And as soon as it's heard,
Not a limb but in discipline's rule is stirred,
And every one sees that those gaily-clad men are all
Ready to die at the word of their general.
(I give him this title, for though it is true
He's a captain alone—of this rifle corps blue—
The intelligent reader will also discern he's
Her Majesty's General—of the Attorneys.)

Away! list again to the trumpet, for hark! it
Sounds gallantly out from the square of Greenmarket.
Away! seek the steps of the classic Town Hall:
See the infantry Rifles respond to the call,
Officers, privates, and bandsmen, and all;
All looking valiant, and all to a man
Determined at least to be found in "the van."

And now cavalry, infantry, all are assembled,
And Greenmarket Square 'neath their tramp has trembled;

And orders of all sorts on all sides are given,
And spurs in the flanks of the chargers are driven—
"March!" "Forward!" Away! "Drive on, coachee!"
    all tell a
Sad tale of what Horace calls *aspera bella*.

   .   .   .   .

The way was long, the day was hot,
The Rifles very warm had got;
Their bright blue coats and silver gay
Seemed to befit a cooler day;
Their swords, their glory and their joy,
Hung in their sheaths, a useless toy;
The first of all the Rifles they
Who rode forth to the Kafir fray.
But, well-a-day! that luck was fled,
No Kafirs were discoverèd:
Though they, the bravest of their race,
Longed to be with them face to face.
No more with hopeful looks they glance,
And spur their steeds to make them prance;
But half their ardour, martial, gay,
In perspiration melts away.

Yet now they make a gallant push,
And bravely scour the scrubby bush.
Woe to the foe that lurks within,
While forward dashes headlong Glynn.
      Woe to the foe!
      "What's that? Holloa!
Somebody's hiding there, I know.
      Huzzah! there he is,
      With his coal-black phiz,

And his black woolly hair too all in a friz:
Yield, villian! yield, or prepare to feel
Two feet and a half of this trusty steel!"

The villian *has* yielded—they've captured him,
And they've tied up his wrists with a bit of a reim—
First fruits of the foray! oh, gallant Glynn,
'Tis thine the honour of war to win.
But what's that remark?
Who talks of a lark?
Do tell us, oh do,
Is it really true?
From trooper to trooper the sentence that's *now* heard,
"The woolly head chap's Mr. Somebody's cowherd."
The gallant captain's seen to smile,
Gravely shakes his head awhile,
Then, as he taps his sabre's hilt, he
Cries, "Let him go! he's found 'not guilty.'"

Forward again in the roasting sun,
Horses and troopers, too, almost done,
March forth the cavalry, one by one;
And behind them the infantry's green coats appear,
For they're still in "the van" though they're still in the rear.

Forward they move, but alas! alas!
Not a Kafir is seen through all the pass
(Though Private Saunders has brought a glass).
Camp's Bay is reached, and each Rifleman's breast
At that moment a thrill of joy confest,
As he gazed on the scene, and half-way up the hill he
Perceived in the distance the round house of Tilley.

And here awhile they rest from labour,
Rifle cast aside and sabre;
At the provisions do their worst,
With beer and soda slake their thirst;
But how they ate and how they drank,
As if each throttle were a tank—
To tell all this my pen would fail;
But even Porter turned to ale.

That night the warrior band returned,
But though their hearts with valour burned,
Not one his spurs as yet had earned.
Though hands were firm and nerves unshaken,
The Kafir foemen had saved their bacon,
And (saving the cowboy) no prisoner was taken.

.   .   .   .   .   .

  The shades of the night
  Had taken to flight,
The sun gave out all his heat and light;
  When some one averred
  That some one had heard
(Or perhaps had been told by some sharp little bird)
  That the fir-trees which grow
  In many a row,
And make 'neath our mountain so pleasant a show,
Concealed in their deepest and darkest recess
The runaway Kafirs who'd made all this mess;
To the terror and horror of those who lived near,
And who hinted they just entertained the slight fear
That between thirst and hunger—a terrible fix—
They might cut people's throats as they'd cut their own
  sticks.

Away at the word goes the valiant crew,
Searching the fir forest right through and through:
"Steady!" cries Captain T——, "steady, men, steady!
Keep your eyes open—be silent and ready."

    Ha, ha, ha! there they go—
    'Tis the foe; 'tis the foe—
But still not an inch of their skins dare they show.
    Bang, bang! goes each gun:
    Helter skelter, too, run
The Rifles, pursuing like mad or like fun—
When some one exultingly cries out "Here's one!"

'Twas true! 'twas one! the ball had sped,
And entered the dying wretch's head;
Forth from the wound the life-blood flowed,
And, stretched in the warriors' very road,
A grisly baboon its carcase showed!
    And the Riflemen stared,
    Half puzzled, half scared,
While a private coarsely remarked, "I'm blowed."
Thus the second day's deeds to an end were brought,
But somehow the Kafirs were *not* yet caught.

   .   .   .   .

    How it turned out next day
    'Twere not easy to say;
But five gallant gentlemen happened to stray
Through the woods for a search, and without any fuss,
Which so often brings forth the *ridiculus mus*,
Pounced right on the runaway Kafirs and bagged them—
That is, on fourteen (quite enough to have scragged
    them);

And this feat all their comrades in arms pronounced
    lucky—
For my part, *I* call it uncommonly "plucky."

And thus ended the Rifle Corps Kafir campaign—
Whose like may the Rifle Corps ne'er see again,
For they'd very much trouble and very small gain.

But Cape Town all felt that, with such an array
Of valour to guard it by night and by day,
    It might sleep in its bed,
    And not trouble its head
About Kafirs in prison, or Kafirs who'd fled.
    For myself I can vow,
    If there's ever a row,
I sha'n't think a bit of the consequence now.
For regular regiments I care not a rap:
The Rifle Corps guards me, what *can* spoil my nap?

A. W. Cole.

AN IDYL OF A PRINCE.

(NOT AFTER TENNYSON.)

    If ever by chance
    You should happen to glance
At a map of the world, and should come upon France,
    Raise your eyes just a bit, un-
    Till you have hit on,
An Island that's known as the home of the Briton.

Now, if it weren't wrong
To put faith in a song,
You would find from a ditty, by one Mr. Campbell,
That one fine day this island
Arose, high and dry land,
Right out of the sea—from no submarine gambol;
But was turned out by order,
Express to afford her
Assistance to Neptune in ruling the ocean,
Which may be the truth, or a mere poet's notion.

Be this as it may—
And I don't mean to say
I have faith in the literal truth of the lay—
She *has* ruled the ocean a pretty long while, and
Is considered a bright little, tight little island;

And, as one thing to brag of,
Possesses a flag of
Such capital bunting, that one Thomas Dibdin
Declared as a fact—and I don't think he fibbed in
The assertion, which every nation allows and hears—
It has braved war and tempest, unhurt, for a thousand
    years.
And, in spite of the seas,
Of the foes and the breeze,
It's as good at this moment as when they first made it,—
Spotless, untattered, and not a bit faded.

To cherish this standard
She has fought, in each land, hard,
But the sea, after all, has been ever her grand card;

And the waves, as they roll
From equator to pole,
Bear fleets on their highway which never pay toll,
Being franked by this banner,
Which waves, in the manner
I've mentioned before, all the breezes that fan her.

I think it an error, to fancy that history
Ever records (when it's truthful) a mystery.
The eyes of a mole
Can't read a large scroll;
They may pick out each letter, but don't see the whole.
The *qui currit potest*
Legere's no test,
As those who have dipped 'neath the surface must know best.
So, though it seems queer
To children who hear
That the tight little island we're writing of here
Has contrived to get on with such brilliant successes,—
Adding conquest to conquest, until she possesses
Much more than old Rome ever ventured to vote as
Her provinces—see *orbs veteribus notus*—
Yet one who reflects
On the matter, detects
All the secret to lie in the fact of the ocean
Receiving his child's never-failing devotion,—
A devotion repaid
By *his* ne'er-failing aid,
So that all the world over,
From China to Dover,
Her fleets defy foeman, and pirate, and rover,
And her shores are as happy as cows are in clover.

Now let your eyes stray
On the map, a long way
From this tight little island, until they make play
Over dreary hot lands
Of deserts and sands,
Where brave Captain Speke
Has set off to seek
For the source of the Nile, till you come, if you'll follow me,
To a country baptized with the name of Cape Colony.
And you'll find, near its south-western corner, stuck down
At the foot of the mountain called Table, a town.

In this town, then, there dwell,
As geographers tell,
A great many people of all sorts of hues,
Heathen, Mohammedans, Christians and Jews,
Dutchmen and Englishmen, black Mozambiquas,
Tawny Malays, and a sprinkling of Griquas,
Hottentots, Kafirs, and Negroes and others,
Who'd be puzzled to point out their fathers or mothers.

They say on the whole that the town's rather pretty
(By the way they've a bishop, so call it a city);
But apt to be sleepy, and stagnant and dull,
In a kind of perpetual calm, or a lull
Of such very long lasting, that no one can form
An idea of the time when it last had a storm.
Now did you ever try on
A slumbering lion
(Of course safe in a cage, or fixed in the wrong hole)
The experiment called stirring up with a long pole?
First you tickle him gently, he stops in a snore,
Then you pummel his ribs and he utters a roar.

Then you give it him harder—a bound and a shake,
A jump at the bars which may well make you quake,
Mane and tail up on end—and the lion's awake.
   Just so they relate
   •How this city of late,
Being sleepy and slow as a solemn debate,
    Was aroused from repose
    By a fly on its nose,
In the shape of a rumour disturbing its doze.
The rumour then spread, and the faster it flew,
The more evident was it the rumour was true.
The city jumped up from its very long snooze,
Threw its nightcap aside, donned its small clothes and shoes,
And was more wide-awake than't has ever been since
It was built—for till now it ne'er welcomed a Prince!
A Prince, then, was coming—a Prince of Blood Royal—
The son of a Queen to whom every one's loyal;
A Prince, too, who wears the triumphant blue jacket,
   To guard from affronting
   That famed bit of bunting,
And pitch into the foe who shall dare to attack it.

A long while the city remained in suspense,
Hopeful, but fidgety, making pretence
    Of not being excited,
   . But looking delighted,
As a boy newly breeched, or a cit newly knighted.
    Grand preparations
    For illuminations.
Fêtes and regattas, and balls and reviews,
Ev'ry one asking, "Well, what's the last news?"

Ladies all crowding, besieging the shops,
Buying dresses so grand that their brilliancy whops
(As Jonathan says) all description, and gloves
And wreaths that they fondly pronounce " perfect loves,"
And lace-bordered lawn for each sweet little nose,
And the finest of pinky-white gauzy silk hose,
And white satin shoes for their dear little toes.

    Volunteers, too,
    Green, scarlet, and blue,
Furbish their uniforms up to look new,
Polish up bayonets, rifles, and sabres,
Looking forward with pride to their arduous labours,
And twist their moustaches with pleasure prophetic
Of how they will look—with the aid of cosmetic.

All things have an end, as experience teaches
(Except crinoline, p'raps, or Upper House speeches);
So at length the suspense was all over—at last
The season of mere expectation was past,
    And in Simon's Bay,
    No very great way
From the city, all snug, the *Euryalus* lay.
    In Adderley Street
    Citizens meet,
Staring at telegrams, hauling out flags,
Stowed safely away in their canvas bags,
Guessing to-morrow will be a grand holiday,
Vowing they'll try, too, to make it a jolly day.
    Cabmen and coolies,
    Whose general rule is

To get in the way when they've got nothing to do,
  Assemble in groups
  At street-corners or stoeps,
And stop up the road when you try to get through.
  And little black boys
  Kick up a noise
By way of evincing their innocent joys.

 . . . . . .

  The morrow came, up rose the sun,
  And who hath seen a brighter one?
  No cloud to obscure a single ray,
  A clear, warm, brilliant summer's day.
  A day right worthy of its scene,
  A people's homage to their Queen,
  In hailing with their heartfelt joy
  Her darling child—her sailor boy!
   The morrow has come;
   Trumpet and drum,
   Streamers and pennants,
   Houses empty of tenants,
   Cannon and bells,—
   Everything tells
   Of a day that's begun
   Of rejoicing and fun.
The city's awake now, as sure as a gun,
And looks almost as bright as that glorious sun.

It's past half-past one, and it's drawing near two—
The hour he's to come, if the programme speak true.
Chevalier Duprat, with his stout bombardiers,
Is preparing salutes to astonish our ears.
The Rifle Corps, too, with their dark-green and black,
Looking regular heroes, and shooters called "crack,"

With their soldier-like colonel—right man in the right place,
Though the steed that he rides isn't such as he *might* grace—
Line the streets in full force,
With also the horse,
Than whom none would fight more—
The brave blue and white corps,
With helmets of silver—such regular shiners—
And the scarlet and gold of the sappers-and-miners.
And last, but not least, with their breeks in zigzag stripes,
The gallant Scotch corps, with their capital bagpipes.
To these add the regulars—regular bricks—
The brave Fifty-ninth, with its flag inscribed LIX.
(And so it does everything—pardon the pun,
It's atrociously bad, but it's true as the sun.)

  At length one hears,
  From the bombardiers,
The banging of cannon, which serves for their cheers;
And the Prince with his retinue really appears
Over Castle-bridge, past Caledon Square,
Of all, save stones and mud-holes, bare.
Beside the parade, with its stunted firs,
Which scarcely the sign of a breeze now stirs,
Through a street where the breeze pretty frequently plays her part,
Now known as Darling Street—*ci-devant* Keizersgracht.

The Prince had arrived, and no princely race
Showed ever a nobler youthful face;
So full of beauty, so full of grace,

His chestnut hair, his large blue eye,
His features calm, wherein seem to lie
Gentleness, intellect, majesty.
A prince right worthy his royal name,
His lineage proud, his father's fame;
Right worthy to wear the glorious blue,
And fight 'neath the banner of England too—
The mightiest banner that ever flew!

      And the motley crowd
      All shouts aloud,
      "Huzzah" and "hooray,"
      And "*Daar komaan hy.*"
And they bless him, and praise him, and most of them pray
That the time may arrive, when he's got to majority,
He may come here and handle the reins of authority.
      Some people, it's true,
      Are inclined to look blue,
For they don't see a crown, and they fear it's a "do;"
      And they're hard to convince
      That a real royal prince
      Isn't born with a crown
      Firmly wedged down
      To the top of his skull,
      Like the deck of a hull;
But he sits on his horse like a prince, like a man,
Sits as only a thoroughbred Englishman can.

In Adderley Street a big archway is seen,
Symbol of triumph, and smothered in green,
Flags waving gaily above it, and near
Crowds of all sorts of people to see and to cheer;

    Then coming next on
    The house of the sexton,
    Past the church, and the banks,
    And the building that ranks
Midst the finest of Cape Town attempts architectural,
Though the order that claims it is purely conjectural,
    Up to the gateway
    At foot of the straight way
Of oaks now all leafless, and passed the Museum
With its curious contents (if the Prince could but see 'em),
To Government House, where His Highness alights,
And sees, lucky Prince, the best sight of all sights,
Such a bevy of fair ones, in costumes so neat,
All murmuring, "How handsome! how charming! how sweet."
I doubt whether prince ever had such a treat.

And next the reception! How tell of the pushing,
The fishing out cards, and the squeezing and crushing,
The bows that are made and the looks that are given,
The gorgeous "get ups" of those who have striven
To display their own grandeur as well as their loyalty,
By wonderful ties to astonish young royalty!
    And the ladies, the dears,
    Abandoning fears,
    Leaving benches outside
    Through the windows they glide,
Rush into the chamber like fairies demented,
Resolved to be present—though not yet presented.
    And all the men swear,
    And the ladies declare,
The former "by Jove," and the latter "'pon honour,"
That to look on that handsome young face is a *bonheur*,

So great that they feel at that moment they doubly can
Pity a people that's only republican.

   The sun's gone to bed,
   And gas lamps instead,
   And lamps blue, white, and red,
   Such a flood of light shed
As drive notions of darkness clean out of your head.
   Pictures, devices,
   Like very large slices
From very large twelfth-cakes, illustrate the crisis.
A lady of very extensive dimensions,
With a helmet and spear of most warlike pretensions,
   But without crinoline,
   Is everywhere seen
Sitting down on her shield by a sea very green;
   And lending a hand
   To assist to the land
A tall, thin, blue gentleman, dressed very grand.

   And one in an able way
   Represents Table Bay,
And a very large dolphin with greenest of tails,
And fins up on end, p'r'aps to serve him for sails,
And another blue gentleman stuck on its back,
Though you'd fancy yourself you'd be off in a crack
If you ventured to sea on so fishy a smack.
   And mermaids are there,
   .With long flowing hair,
And their scaly green tails sticking up in the air;
And Neptune with trident, with mighty long beard,
Hails a nice little midshipman, looking half "skeer'd."
Stores, mansions, and shops—all's a blaze of bright light,
And crowds—black, white, tawney—look on with delight

   Save where the long range
   Of the Merchants' Exchange
Is all in the dark, and the people that stare up
Hear that somehow the electric light *won't* give a flare-up.

   There's the morning gun!
   There's the rising sun!
Put out all the lamps—the fun's over and done.
The city's done all that a good city can,
For one day, at least, has turned out to a man.
There's more work before her of much the same sort,
All sorts of revelry, all sorts of sport.
But my muse for a time flits away from these shores
To take breath, or, more *nauticè*, "lie on her oars."
   But she cries,
   As she flies
   To her home in the skies,
As she ever shall cry till her good lungs shall fail her,
"Hail, Son of Victoria! hail, Royal Sailor!"

     MORAL.

   By the way, as she flew,
   I may say, *entre nous*,
Something fell from her pocket: it looked like a screw
Of tobacco; but though she's got capital jaws,
I never yet found that her ladyship "chaws."
I picked it up carefully, undid the roll,
And found nothing in it except a small scroll,
Which is just in these words—for what I thought a
  "quid" is—
"Happy the Nation Whose Princes Are Middies!"

        A. W. Cole.

A CHRISTMAS APPARITION.

A BIL-IOUS LEGEND.

The day was long sped,
The stars overhead
For three hours or longer their glimmer had shed,
Since the sun had retired remarkably red,
As if the Atlantic had flown to his head,
When Timothy Tadpole turned into his bed.

It was Christmas night,
And a beautiful sight
Was each little star with his modest light,
As if half afraid
Of lending his aid
To the glorious canopy heaven displayed.

Mr. Timothy Tadpole had dined that day
In the ancient and orthodox Christmas way,
Turkey and sausages, roast beef and ham,
Plum-pudding and mince-pies, he'd managed to cram,
With custards and syllabubs, jellies and jam;
And claret and sherry,
And champagne in very
Large glasses, which every one voted the right tap;
. And port which they dish up,
And call it a "bishop,"
With lemons and nutmegs * by way of a "nightcap."

---

* 'Tain't nutmegs at all. Oh what ignorant coves
These authors is! Bishop's port: lemon and cloves.
Printer's Devil.

   And many a toast,
   From the health of the host
To the health of the fair one each tippler loved most,
He had drunk, with a swallow few mortals can boast—
   And "Hip, hip, hooray!"
   He had shouted that day
In a highly excited convivial way,
'Mid Bacchanal ditties, and protests of scorning
To think of retiring to rest before morning.

So when Timothy Tadpole turned into his bed
An ill-natured chronicler might p'r'aps have said
That he carried a little too much in his head—
An uncommon event, too, since Timothy's brains
Were computed to weigh such a very few grains
That in Timothy's head you'd have found them as soon
As a pair of dried peas in the Nassau Balloon.

   And while Timothy lay,
   In a restless way,
Turning, and twisting, and kicking, and rolling,
   That you couldn't suppose
   He'd a bit of repose,
The bell of St. George's was grimly tolling!

Slowly, deeply, boomed the bell—
Midnight hour! it seemed the knell
Of hopes, joys, griefs, pains, pleasures dead,
Gone with the short-lived day that was fled;
Another day from the tiny span
That makes the weal and woe of man!

Yes, twelve at night—
That hour of fright
When ghosts pop out of their graves in white,
And glide and slink
Through keyhole or chink,
Or up the chimney or down the sink;
And frighten poor sinners, who quake as they tell
Of the terrible sight—and the brimstone smell!

As Timothy snored, and kicked, and rolled,
And the bell of St. George's grimly tolled,
Just as the last stroke died on the air
The candle emitted a bluish glare,
(For gentlemen coming home late at night
Often forget to extinguish the light;)
It flickered, and spluttered, and out it went
With a pop, and a hiss, and a nasty scent.

And as it went out a ghost walked in!
An orthodox ghost, with a churchyard grin;
From the head to the feet
Wrapped in a sheet
As white as pure snow—so that, if a man *can* guess,
You'd fancy the ghost had a capital laundress.

Yet the ghost, though pale, wasn't lanky or lean,
Like all ghosts that I've ever yet heard of or seen,
But had rather a corpulent, greasy, fat look,
Like an alderman's ghost, or the ghost of a cook.

As the ghost walked in poor Timothy woke,
And the ghostly vision on Timothy broke;

And Timothy's eyeballs glare and stare,
And up on end goes Timothy's hair,
And Timothy shivers with agitation,
And his body's quite damp with perspiration—
A common effect of consternation.

But as he lies quaking and shivering, still,
      With a resolute air,
      He cries, "Who's there?"
And the vision solemnly answers "Bill!"
Bill! Bill who? Bill Smith? Bill Jones?
For Bill's a prænomen each family owns;
So Timothy tries with might and main
To guess which Bill, but all in vain;
Till, shaking with horror through and through,
He faintly stammers out "Bill who?"

The ghostly accents seem to fill
The room as they answer, "Christmas Bill!
I'm the ghost of the butcher's bill! nothing can lay me:
I'll haunt you by day and by night till you pay me!"

Timothy Tadpole groans with fright,
And tries to shut out the horrid sight,
When lo! a new ghost pops into light;
And the ghost that now burst on the wretched sinner
Was very much paler and very much thinner
(Though afterwards Tadpole remarked it as "rum," he
Spoke in a voice that was husky and crummy).
As solemn and grave as an undertaker
He stalked forth and said, "*I'm* the bill of the baker;
I'll dog you by night—I'll settle your hash—
I'll never be still till you hand out the cash."

Again poor Timothy Tadpole groans,
And turns and wriggles his weary bones,
Trying to shut out the dreadful vision—
When, alas and alack! there's a *new* apparition!

This ghost had an air so dapper and nice, he
Looked for a spirit uncommonly spicy;
But he turned a pitiless glance on Tim,
As if with a look he'd annihilate *him*,
And in accents severe cried, "I'd have you to know, sir,
That *I* am the Christmas bill of the grocer!
You've eaten and stuffed, and you've had your fill,
And now let us see what you've got in the till:
I'll polish you off in a manner that I know
If you don't pretty speedily fork out the rhino!"

But alas and alack! a new one appears,
The tailor's bill, armed with the goose and the shears,
And the bill of the bootmaker, gliding together;
  The latter quite "larking,"
  And pertly remarking,
"Come, dub up, old fellow, there's nothing like leather."
And the bill of the wine merchant, troubled with hiccups,
And the bill of the hosier for collars called "stick-ups."

  And round about his bed they flew
  . Hand in hand, this ghostly crew;
  And they tweaked his nose,
  And tickled his toes,
And rained on his cheeks hard pinches and blows;
And seemed to suppose it a capital lark, as
They stamped and jumped on his aching carcase.

   And aye as they went,
   The air was rent
With their shouting and yelling, and thus they gave
  vent:—
   "Pay us you must,
   Down with the dust;
   None of your "kites,"
   We *will* have our rights;
We'll plague you and pinch you by days and by
  nights;
We'll grind you, and bind you, and force you to
  settle:
None of your promises—out with the metal!"

And Timothy vows that he ne'er heard before as
Awful a noise as this terrible chorus!
He writhed and he wriggled, he twisted and turned;
His tongue was on fire—his head, how it burned!
He struggled and kicked, gave a desperate roar
And a plunge—and came heels over head on the floor.
   The chorus is done:
   One by one
The ghosts have slipped off, having finished their fun.

And Timothy creeps into bed again,
Free from his terror, but *not* free from pain.
The shades of the night like the spirits are flitting,
Grey dawn on the tops of the mountains is sitting,
And under the window a small bantam cock
Is crowing—in fact, it is just four o'clock,
As Timothy, spite of his terrors and bruises,
Yawns, shakes up his pillow, and placidly snoozes!

MORAL.

Don't drink like a fish, and don't feed like a glutton;
Don't forget to cash up for your beef and your mutton,
Your bread and your sugar, your wine and your Allsop;
In short, *all* your bills, and I hope they're a small crop.
    If a tradesman you rob
    You act like a snob,
And you'll find out, moreover, you've done a bad job.
    So seize on the present,
    Pay up and look pleasant;
Think of Timothy Tadpole—that terrible sight there—
A legion of bills makes a deuce of a nightmare!

A. W. Cole.

FREEDOM'S HOME.

T ELL me, where is Freedom's home?
In forest wild—on ocean's foam,
  Amidst the laughing air
    Of sunny skies?
  Or is it where
    The soft voluptuary lies
In rich luxuriousness 'neath marble dome?
Or does it dwell by moss-grown cell
  Where the lone hermit woos the sylvan glen,
Deeming his mind, in solitude enshrined,
  Blest with its happiness afar from men?

    Tell me, which is Freedom's path?
    Where the step no limit hath,

    As lightly borne along
      The smiling earth
    Man tunes his song
      To soul-enamoured mirth,
Devoid of care and undisturbed by wrath?
Or when with schemes enwrapt in dreams
  The young enthusiast on Hope's golden wings,
By love inspired and ardent fancy fired,
  Replenishes life's cup from pleasure's springs.

    Tell me, then, does Freedom's spell
    Revel in the battle's knell,
      When the trumpet's tone
        Betokens death,
      And a soul is gone
        In every passing breath,
Whilst war's loud clangour drowns each wild farewell,
When o'er the grave of the fallen brave
  Memory's bright tribute echoes Glory's claim?
And was the cause, which sought the world's applause,
  Inspired by Freedom's or Ambition's aim?

    Tell me, where does Freedom's cry
    Raise its purest notes on high?
      Oh, not within the halls
        Where Faction's tongue
      Excited calls,
        As if th' appeal it rung
Would burst the bonds of every social tie.
The brightest claim to lasting fame
  Is when in spirit, fired with honest pride,
The patriot's deed stirs nations to be freed,
  As when a Hampden fell, or Sidney died.

Freedom, where is then thy home?
Eye may range and steps may roam,
  And splendour vaunt its joys,
    And he whose breast
  The false world cloys
    In solitude feel blest,
And fancy sport with some ideal gnome;
The pride of might, in war delight,
  When the earth, bloodstained, rings with victory,
But, amongst all, who on thy spirit call,
  Burns there a pure and sacred love of thee?

  Freedom, thou of name sublime,
  Born coeval with all time,
    Can riches, arms,
      Or power impart
    Thy courted charms,
      Unless the human heart
Insures thy smiles unsullied with a crime?
As when the soul from earth's control
  On the bright wings of Faith mounts up on high,
And offers prayer, in humble hope,—for where
  God's spirit dwells, oh, there is Liberty!

G. L.

THE GALLANT "TEUTON."

A TEAR let us give for the gallant "*Teuton*,"
  And bewail the unfortunate dead,
And a wail let us raise for the friends that are gone,
  As they sleep in their watery bed.

A wild shriek rings forth from the crowded deck,
    Borne aloft on the wings of the breeze,
And a cry of despair lingers over the wreck
    As she sinks to her berth in the seas.

The screaming sea-mew plumes his wings o'er their head,
    As he rides at his ease o'er the wave,
While the wailing sea-gull swoops down o'er the dead,
    And sports on their watery grave.

And the ravenous shark from his cave of gloom
    Hurries forth through the dark ocean's depth,
And frolicking round their wave-hidden tomb,
    He gloats o'er the havoc of death.

Then a tear let us shed for the gallant "*Teuton*,"
    And bewail the unfortunate dead,
While the screaming sea-mew sings their funeral song,
    As he rides o'er their watery bed.

H. Hartwell.

THE SUNNY HILLS OF AFRICA.

The sunny hills of Africa, how picturesque and grand,
While clothed in mist the vales lie hid, like some dark spirit-land
The mountains in the distance seen, like hoary castles rise,
And banks of clouds suspended hang, like icebergs in the skies.

The flowery fields of Africa, how beautiful and gay,
The fairest blossoms deck the plains, and perfume fills
 the May,
While gushing streams from every kloof spread o'er the
 verdant green,
And browsing game upon the lands add beauty to the
 scene.

The country homes of Africa, where are their equals
 found?
A welcome always greets the ear, and gladness reigns
 around;
And as one cosily reclines upon the snow-white fleece,
He feels a thrill of thankfulness, of gratitude and peace.

Then should we not love Africa, and speak of her with
 pride,
And hang to her and cling to her whatever may betide?
And though we yield to other lands the palm for scenes
 of mirth,
Our song shall be for Africa—the land that gave us
 birth.

H. Hartwell.

THE SOUTHERN CROSS.

AN ODE.

Thou type of mysteries revealed,
 In man forgiven;
And plainest record of the book unsealed,
 Of starry Heaven!

God's pictured Word, from age to age:
Alike familiar to the child and sage—
In fourfold harmony; like Christ's Evangel page.

How mean to thee this world of sin,
    This atom earth!
Or all the ponderous globes that swing within
    Its astral girth.
Arcturus and his offspring fair—
Where are they? Mazzaroth—Orion, where?
And Pleiades? All, all eclipsed—for thou art there.

'Tis well, when Keills and Newtons write
    With pens of gold;
That ages numberless have winged their flight,
    Myriads untold!
Since thou'st been there; since thou hast taught
How, in His plan, who man's redemption wrought,
That mystery of love was not an afterthought.

Ten thousand worlds have learned of thee
    (Messiah's sign),
What happier eyes were privileged to see
    In Palestine.
But thou, unknown to Eastern seer,
Or king, or priest—we hail with reverence here—
Great harbinger of joy; to this our Ocean-sphere!

So dread we not the wondrous day,
    O holy Cross!
When structures formed of stubble, wood, and hay,
    Shall suffer loss.

When Time's probation shall have past,
And heaven's high starry cope her orbs shall cast,
Even as a tree her fruit, before the felling blast.

For thou immortal ensign bright,
    Art still secure;
When worlds and suns and systems sink in night
    Thou shalt endure.
Endure—Redemption's emblem sweet,
Nor from Creation's altered map retreat,
Nor pass away with noise, nor melt with fervent heat.

Till then, may faith and hope increase,
    Firm, fixed above;
And make us with ourselves at heavenly peace—
    True type of love!
Mid elemental tumults rife
Point us to Him, the Way, the Truth, the Life,
Rock Rimmon of our peace, to heal Baal-tamar's strife.

Stafford Cruikshanks.

HON. WILLIAM PORTER, C.M.G.

AN ELEGY.

THE mighty falls: Time's restless wing
    Has sped the day,
For him!—beloved as Camelot's blameless king—
    To pass away.
And briny tears bedew the date
In which that life so marvellously great,
Our friend—grand Porter's self—succumbs, at last, to Fate.

He died at home: his labour ceased
   Where it began;
While gathering honours, with his years increased;
   Colossal man!
To Africa—that long abode,
His work and love discharged the debt he owed;
Long toil of years—to him—Life's grandest Episode.

The Libyan clime, in youth became
   His destined soil;
Where Time and Fate, the laurels of his fame,
   Can ne'er despoil.
A grateful continent shall pour
Her griefs for him whose face we see no more:
And mourn as great a man as ever touched her shore.

Mourn, soil of grief, your champion bold,
   Whose work is done;
Mourn, land of Ham, as Egypt did of old,
   For Jacob's son.
The mighty falls!—the Chieftain high—
Whose worth not Vaal nor Treasury could buy,
Had reached his native land, and reached it but
   to die.

Approach his grave; oh, sight sublime!
   "Last scene of all."
Let kindred spirits of the olden time
   Attend his pall.
First that Athenian, who alone
In days of tyranny—not since unknown—
With voice of thunder moved the Macedonian throne.

Let Aristides, too, be there—
    The just one still;
'Tis not in Death—on land, or sea, or air,
    Such minds to kill.
Let mighty shades press to the van—
From Cataline's arraigner to the man
Who raised a righteous wail for injured Hindostan.

Let crowding myriads view in tears,
    The hero's grave;
Earth yields to earth: a mortal disappears,
    No love can save.
Lost but to sight; in fame alive,
Long shall his name our blinding tears survive,
And numbers from his dust, true virtue long derive.

Repose, great one, in lasting rest
    Dear friends among;
What rank, what tribe, what country loved thee best
    Remains unsung.
Pride of the Senate and the Bar!
'Tis ours, alas! to wail thy loss afar,
Who 'neath the Southern Cross long hailed thee as a star.

Thou wert our Statesman—to apply
    Wise counsels best;
No selfish partisan to raise a cry
    For East or West.
Prepared for Right to stand or fall—
Deaf to the foeman's threat, or bigot's call—
'Twas thine to live and die, the sire and friend of all.

Who shall succeed thee in our love?
    Who fill thy chair?
Shall we, ignoring succour from above,
    Yield to despair?
No, never, while in hour of need
A champion stands, as he who runs may read—
A Sprigg well worthy power; yea, Porter to succeed.

Stafford Cruikshanks.

ODE ON THE BRITISH SETTLERS' YEAR OF JUBILEE.

NAM QUI HŒC DICUNT, PALAM OSTENDUNT SE
PATRIAM QUŒRERE.

Epoch of hope! Auspicious year;
    Our pride to see;
Hail to thy bright eventful advent here—
    Grand Jubilee!
Since on these shores—our lot was cast,
Of years, seven Sabbaths number with the past;
Thy dawn, O sacred year! proclaim we now at last.

Chime for the Settlers' Jubilee,—
    Spire, turret, fane!
Resound abroad, with quickening ecstasy,
    The proud refrain.
Late, by the Gospel-trumpet called—
O Africa! in Satan's bondage galled,
Shout for the Jubilee, with spirit disenthralled.

Kloof, table-land, and peak sublime,
    Take up the peal;
Chide o'er this wondrous, Heaven-acknowledged clime,
    Man's flagging zeal.
From that far bound, where hope first rose
On Lusitanian Vasco's gathering woes,
To regions far beyond—where Transvaal Jordan flows.

How vast in prospect, mortal man,
    One Spring appears!
In retrospect, how limited the span
    Of fifty years!
Yet gaze around,—how few remain,
Who, in this land, first shared our joy or pain!
Nor doubt we, honoured dead, our loss has been your gain.

Shamgars and Jairs! our heroes true,
    Your types of yore
Gain not by fair comparison with you,
    In heaven-sent lore.
No chief, on Seir's, or Bochim's brow,
Not Gera's son, nor him of "the rash vow,"
In zeal, for cause of right—transcends your glory now.

Your god-like clemency to life,
    In conflicts fell;
The Zeebs and Orebs of each mortal strife,
    Survive to tell.
The ruthless hand, with dagger bared,
In hour of conquest, by your mercy spared,
Has since, as that of friend, your love and bounty shared.

Far better learned your skill to pierce
    The forest King;
Transfix grim Isgram, or the tiger fierce,
    In his death-spring.
Like Kabzeel's Worthy who could dare,
In time of snow, to savage haunts repair,
And slay the monster huge, e'en in his gory lair.

Not gold but prowess then was fame,
    Throughout this land;
True stalwart valour was the test of claim
    To Beauty's hand.
What marvel to acquire such bays,
Each tried to emulate his fellow's praise?
Oh, there were mighty men,—yea, "giants in those days"—

Then learned Moodie, Temlett sage,
    And valiant Graham,
Bequeathed, in turn, to the historic page,
    A lasting name.
As others of no mean degree,
Whose statesmen ken, and iron chivalry
Might worthily attain the rank of "the first Three."

This of the dead,—embalmed in tears,
    In fame alive;
And can we less revere their loved compeers,
    Who still survive?
Ah no! their lives, to many a prayer,
Long, very long, may Heaven benignly spare,
And long each honoured brow its crown of glory wear.

Unwooed, chaste Clio, ever young,
    Descends to save
Her British Settlers from Detraction's tongue,
    And Lethe's wave.
The names of the adventurous few,
Her lamp of Truth displays aloft in view,
Enshrined among the world's regenerators true.

Unutterably fair, behold,
    The goddess bright!
In form and visage of ethereal mould,
    Enrobed in light!
With golden harps—a seraph band,
Less prominent her tuneful sisters stand—
And thus a child of earth receives her high command:—

"Thou, favoured of the Vestal Nine;
    Forensic Cole!
The special delegated task be thine,
    Beyond control;
To celebrate this Jubilee—
In Delphic tones—not uninspired by me,
That envy's self shall mark, for immortality.

Fail not to chronicle a state,
    Beset with woes,
When, like Apollo, on its vision—late
    Wise Porter rose;
Embodiment of Hyde and Hume—
My future Aristides to assume
In every council sway, and change a nation's doom."

It comes! the dawn of brighter times—
    When, to our shores,
The ships of Chittim and remoter climes
    Shall bend their oars!
When Africa, distressed no more,
Shall nobly emulate Columbia's shore,
In European might, and Asiatic lore.

It comes, it comes! ye brethren dear,
    Loud swell the song;
Lo, balmy Abib ushers in the year,
    Expected long!
Illustrious in your thousands come!
High in your ancestors' adopted home,
Raise to triumphal notes the grand memorial dome.

Rouse, Jubilants, by Truth made free,
    Stand ever true;
Nor be your sires Promethean energy
    Extinct in you.
Forget not,—even in Canaan's land,
Though borne to conquest—with a mighty hand,
Your faithfulness to prove—unconquered nations stand.

Thrones raised upon our primal fall,
    Yet mock the skies!
Fierce and unvanquished still,—yea, worthy all
    Your war emprize.
Press, in His cause, expectant on,
Whose sovereign Presence, ever unwithdrawn
Inspires our Faith and Hope, in this Millennial dawn.

Stafford Cruikshanks.

DIVES REDIVIVUS.

'Tis of a rich man near an African hoek,
  Imported from some part of Britain;
You'd say that account in the sixteenth of Luke
  For him, in perspective, was written.

The purple, fine linen, and feasting in state,
  Are all quite in point to the letter;
Save this, that no paupers are laid at his gate,
  Experience has taught them all better.

To lordling and swell, he is all "hand-in-glove,"
  With manners beseeming high station;
Every female in silk has his greeting of love,
  And low bow—and hat salutation.

So much for the wealthy; alas for the poor!
  When one of that number approaches,
Such welcome is found, as the comatose boor
  Reserves for the foe who encroaches.

Our hero has those who describe him indeed,
  'Gainst Vice an unsparing declaimer;
His name it is needless to write or to read,—
  What odds be it Dives or Damer!

You'll stare! he is one who on topics divine,
  Has holiday phrases harmonious;
Right Reverend! how many would fondly incline
  To think the description erroneous!

The pulpit he mounts, as the tyrant his throne,—
  And bawls to the young and the hoary,
With a scowl and a gesture, a stamp and a tone
  Which plainly belie his own story.

Does he toil for a master and home in the skies,
  While in Mammon's vile services flurried!
Pray God that he may never "*lift up his eyes*"
  With the "*rich man*" who "*died and was buried.*"

Stafford Cruikshanks.

THE BURGHERS' GATHERING.

"Fathers, whose sons have bled!
  Sons, who have lost your sires,
Brothers, for brothers dead!
  Arouse your martial fires.
Hurl retribution on the foe
That laid your slaughtered kinsmen low."

Hark! 'tis your country's call
  That swells along the sky;
Come forth, brave Burghers all,
  Responsive to the cry!
I hear the trumpet from afar;
It tells of strife and blood and war.

See! from each vale and glen
    Pour forth the patriot bands—
A host of stalwart men,
    True hearts and steady hands.
Let none be absent from that strife
For home, and liberty, and life.

Long has the combat raged,
    Its war-path marked with blood;
Oft have the troops engaged
    The foe, yet unsubdued.
For yon brave men, it now remains
Yon kloofs to clear,—to scour yon plains.

Arise then in your might!
    Let friend encourage friend;
God will maintain the right;
    To Him your cause commend.
On Him in humble faith rely,
And rush to certain victory.

Burghers! to arms! to arms!
    Haste, mount each trusty steed!
Heed not the Prophet's charms,
    No hostile numbers heed!
On you your country's hopes repose,
Her wrongs to avenge—to crush her foes.

Wide, wide then to the skies
    Your banner be unfurled!
Your patriot enterprise
    Shall ring throughout the world.
Where Britain's standard waves, each land
Shall hear of your heroic band.

Think of the widow's wail,
    Think of the orphan's moan!
Think of each harrowing tale,
    Altars and hearths o'erthrown!
The midnight prowl—the ambuscade—
The traveller's homeward path waylaid!

And call to mind the cries,
    Fervent and numberless,
That shall to Heaven arise
    For safety and success.
Your country breathes one common prayer,
And makes your weal its special care.

And should it prove your lot
    To fill a warrior's grave,
That consecrated spot
    Where sleeps "the fallen brave,"
Watered by grateful tears, shall be
Dear to your country's memory.

Fathers, whose sons have bled!
    Sons, who have lost your sires!
Brothers, for brothers dead,
    Arouse your martial fires!
Pour swift destruction on the foe
That laid your slaughtered kinsmen low.

G. Impey.

GRAHAM'S TOWN,
    October 27th, 1851.

STORM IN TUGELA VALLEY, NATAL.

When once, at ev'ning's mellow close,
   The round moon lit the sky,
And all beneath in calm repose
   In slumber rapt did lie—

Seated on high upon the steep,
   Amid the moonlight glow,
I looked upon a valley deep,
   And on a river's flow.

Sudden, across the chasm wide
   The heavy thunder growled,
While far below in sullen glide
   The noble river rolled.

And now a thousand feet below,
   Betwixt me and the stream,
The thunder-cloud, with lightning's glow,
   Obscures the river's gleam.

Loud and more loud, and all about
   The echoing hills among,
The spirits of the tempest shout
   Their diapason song.

Full in the midst the cloud now parts,
   And wars on different sides,
And through the gap the light moon darts,
   Where bright the river glides.

—— *Moodie.*

Tugela, 1868.

THE NATAL GOLD DIGGINGS.

TO GREENHORNS.

Herr Mauch's all well I dare can tell—
　But don't you go a digging;
The tetse bites, the nigger fights,
　And thieves are always prigging.

The lions growl, the jackals prowl
　All round about the waggon;
And when, poor soul, you seize the bowl,
　You find an empty flagon.

And sleep at night you cannot quite,
　There's such an endless squalling;
Mosquitos sting, hyenas sing
　In human laugh-like brawling.

The zebras bound o'er shaking ground
　In many a wild stampedo;
The blesbok, too, and sportive gnu,
　Make noise as much as they do.

'Fore break of day you must away
　To reach the doubtful water,
And if you're not a steady shot
　You ne'er a buck will slaughter.

So my advice to *Greenhands* is—
　Don't with the goldfields meddle;
But stick to steak and Simms' mild make !
　And " Smouse " around and " peddle."

And those who go—I hope they know
    The lingo of the " Doppers; "
Their customs too, 'twas well you knew,
    To shake them by their floppers.

With stolid stare, your head to bare,
    And answer to each query;
From whence you hail, to where you sail,
    And if your mother's cheery.

In Kaffir *kraals*, look out for squalls;
    Elope not with the "nieces,"
For if you do, the act you'll rue
    Amongst the "Makateses."

Mid upper blacks you'll want an axe,
    For there there's more than one tree;
And gifts a few you'll carry to
    Umziligazi's country.

And now, good-bye, perhaps you'll try
    With crowbar, pick, and hammer,
To soften down stern Fortune's frown,
    And if you can't, why, d———r.

—— *Moodie.*

NATURE.

A DAY ON THE HILLS, IN NATAL.

OF Beauty, Joy, and Life and Light, which dwell
In florid nature, be it mine to tell.
Majestic truth! with Beauty at thy side—
Irradiate maid of highest Heaven's pride;

And thou, undying Harmony, attend,
Romance with fact, and fact with fiction blend.
Bright Virtue bring, by brilliant Fancy drest,
And called by man, Imagination, blest;
That she, companion of the muse, may show
The gentle thoughts that lofty souls should know.

Oh, well do I remember me, when late
I stood upon the beetling crags, to wait
The coming of the rosy-fingered morn,
And view the heavenly tints that thence were born.
Far, far beyond the mountain's pencilled brow,
Defined so clearly in the mellow glow,
Leucothea grey precedes the flaming dye
With which Aurora paints th' orient sky;
Robed in dark shadows lies that mountain now,
O'er which bright phosphor lifts his radiant brow,
While, all above, the leaden-coloured sky
Is cloudless to the little moon on high—
And brightly hangs that little circling moon,
Contrasting richly in that dull cartoon.
But oh, the star! the blazing star above,
The morning and the evening star of love,
Sheds silently upon the scene below
The glowing softness of its ardent brow,
Beams o'er the snowy clouds that calmly sleep
In outstretched slumber on the shadowed steep;
And viewed o'er these, assumes a lurid hue,
But flames the brighter for the contrast too—
E'en so as when along the o'ersnowed ways
Some chilly wanderer wakes the ruddy blaze,
It wears a lustre faint and pale, though bright,
And burns the fiercer in the dazzling light.

Essence of love—a tear by Sappho dropped,
Which Jove, in pity, in its falling stopped,
Suffused with light and his immortal fire
And hung above and granted to inspire
Love's glowing bards, when beauty's chain entwines
The heart that vents itself in am'rous lines.

Now far below, and o'er the shrouded world
Lie, densely clotted, fields of mist enfurled;
Jutting out that molten sea, the rugged peaks
Seem starting into life, to watch the freaks
Of Nature's wildest fancy o'er her glades
That lie embosomed in those fleecy shades—
O'er hills and hills the snowy sheet extends,
And peaceful beauty to the landscape lends;
Hushed is all Nature in her slumber there,
And shrouded are her charms in veil so fair.
Now whisp'ring Zephyrs o'er the changing scene
Are sporting, where so late repose has been,
The mist in circling wreaths departs, nor stays
To idly wanton with the airy fays.
And sternly frowns that dusky mountain still,
And marks their flittings over moor and hill;
Like some fell giant of the early days
Beheld the dancing of the sportive fays.
Oh, for the power of Byron or of Moore,
To glow with one, and with the latter soar;
To find a vent for budding fancy's throes,
And reap the soft luxuriance that she sows;
To snatch a glowing diction's varied strain,
And paint the fire when it flames again;
So I might well portray fair Nature's charms,
Depict the bounties of her lavish arms,

Invoke the strains that to the Nine belong,
And roll the happy tide of thrilling song.

But lo! the rainbow tints that fast succeed
Each other, proclaim th' impatient speed
Of that bright sun that rules our universe,
Of Nature's joys the sole, the constant nurse;
With burning gold he tips those ebon clouds
Whose jagged banks his glory now enshrouds—
Miniature mountains capped with melting snow—
They now appear ere fading 'fore his brow;
The upshot rays he darts through limpid air,
Through half-closed eyes in varied tints appear
The speedy maid, with bow of varied dye,
Throws beaming pleasure in the gladdened eye;
And from this giant peak on which I muse,
All space seems rife with kaleidoscopic hues.
And now Aurora opes the saffron gates,
And all the glory of the sky awakes—
" He flasheth forth like bridegroom to the feast,
Through the red portals of the fiery east."
The glittering dew, with brilliant flashing clings
Around the scattered cobweb's silken strings,
In pearly drops within the lily grows,
Loads the wild violet and the mountain rose;
In silvery sheen arrests each golden ray,
Refracts its stream in multi-coloured play,
As shivered mirrors on a flow'ry lawn
Reflect a thousand tints where one is born,
And filtering through these early morning beams,
Sinks spangling round the smoking mountain streams.

Resuming now my trusty Terry's weight,
I wander on where fleeting game or fate

Does guide my steps—where o'er the sloping grounds
High in the air the exulting Oribe bounds—
"The rifle raised and levelled with the eye,
Sharp a short thunder rolls along the sky,"
Swift to the unconscious hind the leaden death
Speeds on the wings of fate and stops his breath;
With one quick spring he falls upon the plain,
No more o'er vernal lawns to bound again.
Or, where the wary Rhee buck, wild and shy,
Perceive afar the hunter drawing nigh,
Together rush in one affrighted band,
And wildly gaze and tremble as they stand;
Till fully scared, with one short cough, again
They sweep like wind across the sounding plain.
Where, mute and lonely on the impending steeps,
The mountain hawk his frequent vigil keeps,
With noiseless pinion shoots into the air,
And sails upon the wind that's wandering there;
With head oblique he scans his native sky,
Then far below his piercing glances hie
To where his dreaded shade portentous sweeps
O'er wilds, where in the sun the coney sleeps;
With sudden fear the rocks with cries resound,
As dive the furry tribe beneath the ground.
Now down I stray to where yon rushing rill
Is tumbling down the rock-defended hill,—
Here grateful winds in many a whispered lay,
With mild impression o'er my forehead stray,
And here reclined, where shadowed flows the stream,
I lend myself to reverie and dream.

Remorseless Time has rolled long years away
Since last I faced wild ocean's fresh'ning spray,

But still a charmed impression lingers o'er
The heart, when scenes she's often felt before,
Come crowding on her corners, thick as waves
Roll closely sequent into lonely caves;
Which prompts me to retune my feeble lyre,
And sing the theme of which we never tire;—
But whence this thought that thus the past recalls
That sudden gleams and oft the mind appals?
Without the faintest cause or reason plain,
This lightning thought darts quickly on the brain,
Picturing in the clear mirror of the mind
The distant spot that long we've left behind,
In faithful semblance painting on her eye
The bygone scene to mem'ry now so nigh,
And then as sudden flies, unless as here,
We fix the shadow e'er it disappear.
Not ev'ry one has felt this vision leap
With magic bound upon their mem'ry's sleep,
But some there are, who, startled by the spell,
Retain remembrance to the feeling well;
Each spoken word, each gesture will appear
To have been acted in some former year,
And oft we think we almost can foretell
The next words spoken in this passing spell.

But how shall I essay to shape my way
Through themes, that multi-genius 'fore my day,
Has wrought upon and left no point unviewed,
That varied Nature on their minds imbued?
How through exhausted pictures steer my course,
And shun the oft-used terms that almost force
Themselves upon expression, for they deem
They are the *sine qua nons* of the theme,

And cling so firmly in the lab'ring breast,
That 'tis beyond its power to divest
Its chambers of these oft-recurring terms,
That stamp their image and implant their germs.
Coincidence of thought will oft produce
The same in words, and thus I do adduce
That censors ne'er will quibble in these times,
Nor scent a plagiarist in these stray lines.
So bear we on with that we have contrived,
Ne'er pausing to reflect from whence derived,
Nor spurn a passage for the reason that
Its semblance was in other brains begat—
For truth will charm though sung in echoed strain,
And changeless scenes instruct the bard again.

With long-swept rise and swiftly gathering sweep,
That seems to rake the bosom of the deep;
With curling crest and tint of lucid blue,
That glows with innate specks of snowy hue;
With pendent pause and darkly swelling breast,
That heaves as lovely woman's in her rest;
The mighty eastern wave with booming roar
Falls thund'ring on old Afric's rocky shore.
With busy spread he swamps the crannied rocks,
And now refills a thousand puny locks,
In seething eddies swirls and frets about,
Then shrinking back, he sinks, and hurries out.
Recalled, I ween, by some internal power
That guides his motion and directs his hour;
As does the heart, withdrawing in its turn,
The drop it late emitted from its urn.

Now further down along the sandy beach
The waves seem stretching to their utmost reach,
Then swift receding with the grating sand,
They curl in little rills along the strand,
While myriad tribes of sea-born insect life
Pursue their exit and enjoy their strife;
The fresh'ning sea-breeze spreads her airy wings,
And health and coolness to the seashore brings;
The tumbling porpoise bowl along the tide,
And now aloft, now down the billow glide,
And shrieking sea-birds swooping round the steep,
Skim the gay surface of the cresting deep;
The distant ship, as viewed from Komo's cliff,
Seems almost dwindled to a fisher's skiff;
As swiftly gliding o'er the seething surge,
She sinks beyond the horizon's dusky verge;
While flaming in the painted west again,
" The sun's last splendour lights the dazzling main."
Lo! on the flushed horizon rolled along
Dark mountain lines of clouds embattling throng,
Mid blood-tipt peaks of fiercest fiery hue
Intensely sleeps th' unutterable blue;
While gentle Hesperus from the empurpled sky,
Serenely lustrous as repose draws nigh,
Sinks sweetly smiling to her silken bed,
Where gorgeous robes and pillowing folds are spread,
And darkened Day leaves stretching o'er his grave
Deep crimson stains along the dark-blue wave.

My song has wandered from the mountain stream,
And Ocean's wonders still employ my dream,
And here the cherished image of the brain
In pensive beauty shades the heart again;

Fond, foolish fancy, ever hov'ring nigh,
Paints her own idol on the wistful eye,
And breeds an atrophy's insatiate ill,
Which though with nectar slaked, is cheerless still.
Oh, for the witching arts of ancient days,
When mortals, oft transmuted into fays,
Were given to guide the streamlet's winding course,
And dwell enchanted at its bubbling source,
That I an Oread of my love might make,
To bless my steps through hunting glade or brake,
And roam with her where mountain cascades roll,
The guiding star, the Beatrice of my soul.
But to my theme—the sunny hours flow by,
And still unnumbered objects please the eye;
I watch the bubbles in their endless race,
For ever glancing o'er the brooklet's face;
Oft at some sailing bud there sudden leaps
The finny darter of the glassy deeps;
While quiv'ring lilies in the current's sweep,
In dancing movement, ceaseless motion keep;
I watch the butterflies in giddy flights,
Intensely mad, enjoying noon's delights;
They meet, they turn, they hover here and there,
Then wildly scatter through the heated air.

The sun declines, behind the clouds he steals;
Loud o'er my head the sudden thunder peals,
And winged with lightning, awful echoes wakes
In caves rebellowing to the din it makes—
Dies on the breathless air, the song of birds,
And distant low the homeward wending herds;
The twitt'ring birds now seek the leafy brakes,
The lofty eagle now his perch forsakes,—

Forth from his castled rock he sudden flies,
And shuns in caves the fury of the skies.
Now heavy clouds o'ershade the verdant plain,
Then on the thirsty earth descend in rain;
And now the snowy hail, with rushing sound
Falls from its crystal quarries to the ground.
'Tis past! the sun a moment smiles in joy,
And rides his parting course without alloy;
While Zephyrs coy compound a gentle breeze,
And fan the air, and play among the trees.
Sunk o'er the mount, far in the tinted west,
The hidden sun has now declined to rest;
And ling'ring twilight, gloaming o'er the hill,
Sheds softest influence on the evening still.
I fain would cease, yet many thoughts still flow
Upon my mind, though ever waning low,
As when old Ocean's billow-beaten shore
Has echoed to the wakened waters' roar;
The o'erflown storm an agitation leaves
That still the less'ning wavelet on him heaves—
And still these little waves will ceaseless play
As ruling passions ever hold their sway;
Our primal thoughts will ever flow toward
Their consummation of their own accord,
As fountains, scattered o'er a mountain's side
Will still, unto a point, converging, glide.

High on this hill I sound my rugged shell,
And sweep th' untutored lyre; and should I swell
A strain of feelings purer than I feel
In th' envenomed world below, and steal
The precepts of the Ethic muse to sing
Of that I practise not, forgive my string.

For still with joy is hailed the welcome hour
That bears respite from frequent trials' power;
And all the puling prate of fashion's twang,
And jarring accents of the city's clang;
Releasing from the weary humdrum prose
That marks each dreary day's monot'nous close;
And lifts us from the plain of low desires
To where Imagination never tires,
Where Contemplation plumes her ruffled wings,
And th' untrammelled mind beholds all things,
As through a stained and softly coloured glass
One views the dream-like trees and waving grass,
And transports where kind Nature oft bestows
A soothing cup—nepenthe of our woes—
And though the harp be swept by bard profane,
If good the theme, the song is ne'er in vain;
For should his simple lay be nursed by fame,
Old Time forgets the follies of his name,
F' ffaces all the failings of his life,
And rears the strain that softens earthly strife.

And now, farewell!—dark shades enwrap the hill,
O'er dying day the dews in tears distil,
To shine again when with the morrow's dawn
The golden light and joyous sun are born,
As gathered tears called forth by sorrow's night,
In Beauty's eyes, when lit by joy, are bright—
The sable Night, with dusky wings on high,
With silent pace invades the spangling sky—
And distant gleaming on th' horizon's verge,
The parting storm rolls out its solemn dirge—
And should this artless strain a thought afford
That strikes in gen'rous breasts a fellow chord,

Then, oh! forgive, that thus I rashly dare
From Nature's hallowed charms the veil to tear—
But ever with her changing scenes imbued,
Her pleading beauties urge me to intrude.

———— *Moodie.*

MELSETTER, *January* 1868.

CONTENTMENT.

FOR MY MOTHER.

I AM content to be
What God has made me: honour and renown
I seek not from this world, nor fear its frown.
God knows and honours me. His child and heir
He made me; then what matters it if here
Unknown and poor I live,—a little while,
And I shall bask in His benignant smile
      To all eternity.

I am content to do
What God has bid me: He, the Master, knows
What work I am best fit for, and He shows
Me how to do it. *His* command is law;
His the responsibility. In awe
And fear of failure, I seek to *obey*
And leave results to *Him*, and daily pray
      To be more faithful, true.

I am content to go
Where God sees fit to send me: *everywhere*
His presence I can feel, His sweet voice hear,

His footprints see, His guiding hand discern,
His loving-kindness taste, His precepts learn.
Each step, though dark and difficult the way,
Leads me but *nearer* to eternal day—
    Farther from sin and woe.

    I am content to take
Life's good and ill: the hand that holds the rod,
And blessings too, is guided by my God.
He knows best which I need the most, and will
My cup with joy and sorrow wisely fill.
I wish to listen only to His voice
That bids me in prosperity rejoice,
    Or suffer for His sake.

    I am content to wait
Till Jesus calls me home.—'Tis true I long
To join in that celestial, happy throng,
And sing His praise, and see Him as He is,
And taste the joys of ransomed souls in bliss;
But still, resigned I wait at His command
Until He come to take me by the hand,
    And lead me through the gate.

Rev. F. J. Ochse.

BEACONSFIELD.

NOT HERE.

*H*ERE is not the place of rest,
    Where sin and sorrow reign;
Where sighs and tears show that the heart
    Is filled with grief and pain;

Where strength and beauty fade away;
Where flowers bloom but to decay;
Where sweet emotions cannot stay,
   But come to go again.

Now is not the time of rest,
   While work is to be done;
While every moment hastens by,
   And is for ever gone;
While souls are lying in the might
Of Satan, and the shade of night
Is threatening to quench the light
   And leave our work undone.

There in yon firmament on high,
   Amongst the good and blest,
Where angels sing and seraphs praise—
   The brightest and the best—
There will our songs for ever rise
To God, the Object of all eyes,
There we will find in heavenly skies
   The *place* and *time* to rest.

Rev. F. J. Ochse.

REVELATION XXII.

VERSIFIED.

AND He showed me a River, whose life-giving waters
   Are pure and like crystal so clear.
It flows from the throne of the merciful Father,
   And Jesus our Saviour so dear.

In the streets of the City and sides of the river
   The Tree of eternal Life grows ;
Its fruits are all savoury, its leaves are all healthy,
   And healing to every one flows.

No curse shall be found in that city so glorious,
   Where God and the Lamb ever reign ;
There His servants shall serve Him, His children shall see Him,
   His name in their foreheads remain.

No night shall be there,—neither candle nor sunlight,—
   The Lord shall in glory there shine ;
There in bliss they will reign, for the Lord God hath said it,
   The God of the prophets divine.

" Behold, I come quickly, to bless him that keepeth
   The sayings and words of this book ;
Then seal not these prophecies, telling of judgment,
   But let them all into it look.

" The time is at hand, and the unjust shall perish,
   The filthy shall filthy remain,
The righteous shall still with more righteousness glitter,
   The holy his pureness retain.

" Behold, I come quickly, let all this remember,
   My righteous reward is with Me ;
And surely to each one will I give a portion,
   According as his works shall be.

"As I am the Alpha, so I am Omega,—
  The First and the Last and the All;
And he who puts trust in the Offspring of David,
  Shall stand and shall nevermore fall."

The Bride and the Spirit together are saying:
  "Oh, come to Him, thirsty one, come!"
And he who will hear it, and he who will have it,
  May drink of that water from Home.

Once more He who testifieth all these things saith:
  "Surely I will speedily come."
My heart, with a longing response, gives the answer:
  "Even so, Lord Jesus! oh come!"

Rev. F. J. Ochse.

EZEKIEL XLVII. 1–12.

AND I saw a little stream
Come trickling out from underneath the altar;
And as it rippled sunward with glad psalter,
    It sparkled in its beam.

    A tiny stream it was
As it issued from the threshold of its home;
But with growing bulk and power to overcome
The sandy desert, it became at length,
A mighty river, glorious in its strength,
    O'er which I could not pass.

Both its sides were lined with trees
All along its strange course through the desert sand.
Trees of fruit and beauty in a barren land—
Trees with healing in their leaves for every pain—
Trees of fragrant odours floating o'er the plain,
    Borne by the desert's breeze.

Into the sea this stream
With strength and vitalising power flowed,
Till everything new life and vigour showed.
Great multitudes of fish this dead sea filled,
Which of its deadly saltness now was healed.
    Thus ended my whole dream.

And when I woke methought
I saw God's mercy, like this stream,—its source
The Upper Sanctuary—this world its course—
The secret of its healing power, the blood
Poured on the altar under which it flowed,—
    Free pardon Jesus bought.

The Dead Sea's awful gloom,—
Fit symbol of this world of death and sin.
Its new state, with the river pouring in
New life and health, where death and silence reigned,—
Fit emblem of the "paradise regained"
    From sin's eternal doom.

Rev. F. J. Ochse.

CHANGE.

Yes, all things change in this poor world of ours,—
The ocean's waves, the sand upon its shores,
The rocks which bound it even slowly change.
Summer's warm breath makes place for Winter's cold.
Spring's youthful freshness, beautiful and gay,
Is doomed to Autumn's sadness, age, decay.
Life's phases change: now happiness and joy;
Then misery and sorrow take their turn.
Now health and plenty, shared with loved ones near;
Then pain and sickness, poverty, despair,
For the poor, exiled, friendless wanderer.
Now in *this* field, with friends and blessings rich,
The labourer works content; then parting comes,
And to a new and unknown sphere he turns
His wandering steps, and hopes and prays and works.
Friends also sometimes change: the tender flower
Of friendship often withers in the blast
Of cruel, sinful scandal, cursed of God.
Others indifferent grow: pleased by new friends,
The old ones are neglected and forgot.
Yes, all things change in this poor world of ours—
God's love alone remains unchangeable.
His love alone can keep us constant, true.
No blast can wither friendship's tender flower
That blooms beneath His atmosphere of love.
Then let all things in this poor world of ours
Change and decay;—no matter, we have *God*.

His promises are sure, His blessings great;
His faithful guidance will be ever ours.
A place awaits us in His glorious Home,
Where *we* shall also be *unchangeable*.

Rev. F. J. Ochse.

HEAVENLY FRIENDSHIP.

There is a hand, whose grasp is love,
    Though not a lover's grasp;
Its touch wakes feelings far above
    The lover's fondest clasp.

There is an eye, whose sparkle shows
    The tender holy flame
Of deep affection, and o'erflows
    With love for each dear name.

There is a heart, whose throbs proclaim
    A constant, ceaseless flow
Of life and love for all; the same
    In happiness or woe.

A lip, whose words—to man on earth,
    Are words of life and peace;
To God, are prayers of priceless worth,
    Which never, never cease.

Such is our Saviour dear, our Heavenly Friend.
  Most like Him is the mortal friend, who tries
To lead us ever nearer to that land
  Where Friendship blooms in sunny, cloudless
    skies.

Rev. F. J. Ochse.

LINES WRITTEN IN AN ALBUM.

FROM whence comes all this weariness of heart,
This anxious longing for a place of rest,
These greedy cravings for the silent tomb,
Where all in deep forgetfulness repose?
Surely man was not made to while away
His costly time in brooding over wrongs
And disappointments meeting him through life,
As if there were no rays of sunshine left
To gladden him along his way to Heaven.
His life is not an empty, idle dream,
But dread reality, composed of *facts*,
Whose fruits will follow with their just rewards.
He *has* an object which to live for here;
And if that object be to live for God,
And for the good of those who him surround,
He may consider his a life well spent.
Then let us follow firmly duty's call
With willing hearts, forgetful of the past,—
Still trusting in the strength and love of God,

Still striving further onward for the crown,
Still rising higher heavenward to our goal,
Till we at last that longed for Home attain,
And rest upon the bosom of our God.

Rev. F. J. Ochse.

THE DEFENCE OF RORKE'S DRIFT.

JANUARY 22–23, 1879.

COME listen for a moment,
  All ye, whose peaceful life
In even flow is ne'er disturbed
  By scenes of blood and strife;
Who sit around your hearth fires,
  Secure from war's alarms;
This humble lay sets forth to-day
  A British deed of arms.

Left on the wild, lone border,
  A small but fearless band,
Guarding the watery entrance
  To savage Zululand;
On the warm mid-day breezes,
  Like thunder's distant sound,
Came the long roll of cannon
  Far o'er the hostile ground,
And we wondered that our column
  So soon the foe had found.

Then came two flying horsemen
  Riding with loosened rein,
And the powdery dust like a whirlwind rose
  As they scoured across the plain;
A few more rapid hoof-strokes,
  And we heard the news they bore—
"In yonder glen nigh half our men
  Lie weltering in their gore!

"'Twas shortly after noontide,
  The column was away;
Swept the dark hordes in myriads down
  Like wolves upon their prey;
Vainly the deadly hailstorm
  Boomed from the cannon loud—
Vainly we tried to stem the tide
  Of the black surging crowd.

"Our men, too soon surrounded,
  Were slaughtered as they stood,
Facing their slayers to the last,
  Dying as soldiers should.
How we escaped we know not,
  From that fierce whirlwind's frown,
But on this post a conquering host
  E'en now is marching down!"

As men who dream, we heard them,
  And awestruck, stood aghast;
And through each heart there went a chill
  Like the breath of an icy blast;

We thought of those who left us
   In the glow of their martial pride,
Now with the dead in the slaughter red,
   Stark on the wild hill-side.

We looked to our defences
   Ere darkness should come on,
And others passed from the fatal field,
   They warned us, and were gone;
We called on them to aid us
   In the approaching fight—
They would not hear—the voice of fear
   Lent wings to their headlong flight.

"The foe comes down in thousands,
   Away—for all is lost!"
"Not so—our orders are to hold
   The Drift at any cost;
Long has the firing sounded
   And succour may be nigh,
If not—why then we're Englishmen,
   At duty's call we'll die!"

We set to work undaunted
   To raise a barricade,
With mealie bags and scattered stores
   A breastwork soon had made;
And scarcely was it finished,
   When burst upon our sight,
Dark as the lowering storm-cloud
   Sweeps the blue vaulted height,
Moving along the fair hill-side,
In vast black lines extending wide,

Rank upon rank of warriors tried,
In panoply of savage pride
   Advancing to the fight.

Above the dusky phalanx
   We marked each ring-girt head,
We felt the hard earth tremble
   Under their heavy tread,—
The martial tread of thousands
   In full array of war—
Each sinewy frame well trained to wield
   Broad assegai and tufted shield,
Washed upon many a hard-fought field
   In vanquished foeman's gore.

Yes, on they come in thousands—
   One hundred strong we stand,
Against the very pick and flower
   Of warrior Zululand:
And how may we resist them,
   Or hope to hold our own,
Flushed as they be with victory—
   The greatest e'er they've known?

They pressed in silence forward
   At a swift but steady run,
Red glowed their blades in the golden beams
   Of the declining sun;
With gliding undulation,
   On, on their masses came—
A mighty crash—a lightning flash—
   Streamed the death-dealing flame.

Still the black wave rolled onward—
    Again the word rang out,
With the sharp volley's crackling voice
    Arose a deafening shout :
Blent with the rush of thousands
    Over the rumbling ground,
The battle-cry pealed to the sky,
    Starting the echoes round.

'Tis long since that wild slogan
    Rallied these bands to war,
The dreaded hosts of Zululand
    Now in the field once more;
Oft have the neighbouring tribesmen,
    At the blood-curdling tone,
Awoke in the calm still hours of night,
To flee by their blazing kraals' red light,
    To forest thickets lone.

'Neath far Quathlamba's ridges
    Cut clear against the sky,
Where now, upon those grassy slopes,
    Snug homesteads nestling lie;
As sweeping down resistless,
    A black o'erwhelming flood,
The ruthless hordes fell on their prey,
And broad their dark destroying way
Was long mapped out, for many a day,
    By ruins soaked in blood.

Their forward van all shaken,
    They wavered—then fell back—

Bestrewn with dark grim corpses
   Was all the gory track:
They turned to seek for cover,
   They'd seen what we could do,
And overhead, with angry whiz,
   Like hail their bullets flew.

And by their hosts surrounded,
   Nigh forty men to one,
We vainly scanned the darkling waste
   Ere twilight should be done;
As waif on the wide ocean,
   Looks for the rescuing sail,
When dim shades sweep the surging deep,
   And louder roars the gale.

Behind the western ridges
   The sun's red lamp sank down,
The twilight shadows seemed to cast
   O'er all a threatening frown;
We gazed with mingled feelings
   On the last-fading beam,
Should we, too, lie 'neath the cold grey sky,
   Stark in the dawning gleam?

We looked at one another,
   Then at the purpling west,
Then came the thought of our noble trust,
   Filling each soldier breast;
And there, that trust defending,
   We'd perish as we stood—
Telling of death seemed the night-wind's breath,
   Heavy and dank with blood.

Again the thrilling war-cry
   In wild shrill notes rang out,
Again th' infuriate mass bore down
   Upon our frail redoubt;
They poured their swarming numbers
   Over the barricade—
But one short stand, our gallant band
   That first mad onslaught stayed.

Yet fiercer still and bolder
   They rushed into the fight—
When to the smoke-beclouded sky
   Shone a dull reddening light:
With a chill of consternation
   We marked the lurid glare,
Knowing that then our wounded men
   Were helpless lying there.

Then from the glowing furnace
   We brought them one by one,
But the foe closed up too quickly,
   Ere half our work was done;
We faced the yelling masses,
   We braved the crackling fire,
Till through the smoke the fierce flame broke,
   Forcing us to retire.

The cruel demons entered,
   All eager for their prey,
The helpless sick and wounded
   Were butchered as they lay;
As the huge flames roared upward
   With red and hungry light,
In the fierce glare that met us there—
   Stood all revealed the fight.

Widened the glowing circle
  Crowded with clamouring bands,
All weirdly shone the flashing blades
  Brandished by grisly hands;
Again, again upon us,
  Poured the dark howling flood,
Quivered the ground beneath their bound,
  Red with our comrades' blood.

We thought of these comrades butchered
  As they unresisting lay;
We ceased to give a passing care
  To the issue of the fray;
We only longed for vengeance
  On all the fiendish crew,
To let them feel our British steel,
  To strike both oft and true.

The flaming pile sank inwards
  With a roar like thunder's tone;
Arose a sickening stench of blood
  And many a gurgling moan;
Still the terrific war-cry
  Blent with our furious shout,
Harder they pressed upon us—
  Quicker we drove them out—
Hurling them back in the gory track,
  Upon the clamouring rout.

And eyes with lust of carnage,
  Like coals through the darkness gleamed,
And bayonet crashed with stabbing spear,
  Thick the red torrent streamed:

Drowning the roar of battle—
   Drowning the deafening clang—
Each demon yell, like a blast of hell,
   Fiercer and higher rang.

Still the bright volley's flashing
   Showed the wild frenzied crowd,
Their shields and spear-hafts clashing—
   Their war shouts pealing loud—
And myriad eyeballs glowing,
   Like starlit ocean tossed—
And blood, like water, flowing,
   When splintering weapons crossed.

Our bayonets blunt and twisted,
   All dripping black with gore;
And many an open bleeding gash
   Its own grim witness bore;
Our brains all faint and dizzy,
   Our throats all parched with thirst,
At every shot our guns grew hot
   As though about to burst.

Again, again, we met them
   Through the long fearful night;
We fought as ne'er we fought before
   And ne'er again may fight,
To 'venge our slaughtered comrades,
   To guard our solemn trust,
And to reclaim our country's name
   Trampled in savage dust.

We stood upon our rampart,
   As paled the morning star,

We saw the baffled foe retreat
    Over the hills afar;
The long night's deadly struggle
    Seemed like a troubled dream—
Our peril passed, new hope at last
    Came with the dawning gleam.

Piled high against our breastwork,
    And scattered o'er the plain,
Four hundred of their warrior strength
    Lay stark amid the slain—
Lay where their fierce hot lifeblood
    The greedy earth had wet—
Still terrible, in threatening scowl,
    Each grim dead face was set.

Our strength and ammunition
    Alike were well-nigh spent—
On an approaching dust-cloud
    Our eager glance was bent,
There moving slow and rising,
    Far in the hostile land,
Till, through the haze, our straining gaze
    Descried an armèd band.

Is it the foe returning,
    'Gainst us in greater strength?—
We watched the distant column
    Deploying in its length:
Hurrah—the British scarlet
    Gleams in the morning sun—
We'll see once more old England's shore,
    Her thanks we've fairly won.

Yes, for old England's honour
    And for her perilled might,
We strove with vast and whelming odds,
    From eve till morning light;
And thus with front unflinching,
    One hundred strong we stood,
And held the post 'gainst a maddened host
    Drunken with British blood.

And twelve from out our number
    Their brave career had run,
Their final muster-roll had passed,
    And their last duty done;
So carefully we laid them
    Deep in the green earth's breast,
An alien sod above them trod;—
    Peace with their ashes rest!

Her sons, in gallant story,
    Shall sound old England's fame,
And by fresh deeds of glory
    Shall keep alive her name;
And when, above her triumphs,
    The golden curtains lift—
Be treasured long, in page and song,
    The memory of RORKE'S DRIFT.

Bertram Mitford.

"RORKE'S DRIFT."

JANUARY 22, 1879.

On the wild river's bank two horsemen appear,
They are bearers of tidings that fill them with fear;
" Haste, put us across, and prepare for the fight,
The Zulus are out in their uttermost might;
They rushed on our camp like a dark hungry flood,
And their spears are all red with our countrymen's blood."
   " Hurrah, we will fight for Old England."

We heard them, a moment our pulses stood still,
Then went we to work with a heart and a will—
Two stores to defend—with a hundred, all told,
And thirty sick mates. "Come, boys, let's be bold;
Let's fasten the waggons together with chain,
And build up our ramparts with sacks full of grain."
   " Hurrah, we will fight for Old England."

What is that coming on like a herd of black game,
Round the hill to the south, with the speed of a flame,
With feathery plumes like wild manes flaunting high,
And a sound like a myriad wings in the sky?
The *Zulus!* for now in the sun's glance appears
The quivering lightning-like sheen of their spears.
   " Now, boys, let us fight for Old England."

They are on us! Six hundred at first, with wild cries—
The lust of the battle still red in their eyes—
The blood of our comrades still wet on each blade,
And see! there come thousands behind to their aid—

But, thanks to the heads that directed our hands,
All firm and unbroken our little camp stands.
   "Hurrah, we will fight for Old England."

It stands like a rock the Atlantic's wild wave
Breaks over and harms not.—We took and we gave—
They leapt on our "walls" with stab, hiss, and yell—
They came on in thousands, dark legions from hell!
Our bayonets were ready, our rifles were *there*,
And their small tongues of flame spoke of death in the air!
   "Hurrah, how we fought for Old England."

They took half our fort—foot by foot—inch by inch—
They lighted the roof, and yet none would flinch;
We threw up another redoubt with the maize,
And fought by the light of the hospital blaze
When the darkness came down—and all through the night
Surrounded, we kept up the terrible fight.
   "Hurrah, how we fought for Old England."

Ah! who shall declare what brave deeds were done,
Ere the world woke again to the light of the sun?
For twelve long, long hours we stood at our posts,
And beat back, how often! the enemy's hosts.
We had our revenge for the blood that was shed,
At dark "Isandhlwana"—*they paid for our dead.*
   "Hurrah, how we fought for Old England."

Day broke, and the devils had silently gone,
We counted their dead, more than twenty to one!
Our loss was Fifteen—so we set up a shout
That frightened the vultures slow sailing about.

   .   .   .   .

In the heart thrill of nations will live your reward,
Oh! brave "Twenty-fourth," oh! brave Bromhead and Chard—
"Hurrah, how you fought for Old England."

A. Brodrick.

PRETORIA, 1882.

BEFORE ULUNDI.

WE had to retreat, entirely by Zulus surrounded—
We had to retreat, but we cut our way through as you know.
Bold Beresford lingered, while loudly the bugle was sounded,
And turned in his saddle to take a last look at the foe.

A trooper's horse dropped; its rider lay stunned for a minute—
But quick as the lightning the storm-cloud in summer reveals,
A voice cried, "Come, quick! see the stirrup—now set your foot in it—
And jump up behind, for the devils are close to our heels."

"No, here I'll remain. Go on, and don't mind me, your honour,
Ride on, save yourself, if I'm killed I shall never be missed."
But the mare had to carry that day double burden upon her—
"Come up, or by heaven, I'll give you the weight of my fist."

Then away went the mare, and many a yell from pursuer
Rose high on the air while fast o'er the wild veld they fled,

No braver heart beat on that day, no braver or truer
Than his whose strong arm snatched a comrade from
 realms of the dead.

Ere sundown they rode into camp and quickly dis-
 mounted,
And then they shook hands and parted, "To arms!" was
 the call.
Of all the good deeds that were done, oh! shall not be
 counted
Bold Beresford's ride with the Sergeant the bravest of all?

A. Brodrick.

Pretoria, 1882.

THE BARON'S ADVENTURE.

(A FACT.)

Voici une pétite chanson
Pour le Baron de Sanson
A story—a tale, what you call episode—
On the trials he meet
Wiz his cart (de visite)
On ze laissez-faire, what you call Idle-burg Road.

You know how he state
Dis country is great?
And most be duv-velop, c'est vrai, it is true—
Vel, listen my story—
I tell con amore,
Ze Baron he nearly vos duvvel op too.

Ze chemin vos von mud,
Ze rain vos ze vlood,—

He arrive by ze river, ze water vos "grand,"
His friend look to him
And say, "Can you swim?"
Zen jomp comme un poisson and sit on ze land.

Mais le Baron vos tumble,
He make one big jumble,
And mix vis ze buggy and turn razzer pale,
And ze friend, he that voss up
Say to me, "It's von toss up
What side is ze Baron, ze head of ze tail?"

We make a big screamin',
Zey fling a big reim in—
Zey catch ze brave Baron—comme ça—par la jambe—
Ze clothes vos departed,
He sigh, zen he started—
And after some cognac he say, "Vare I am?"

Ah! but he vos plucky,
He say he vos "lucky"—
He vos bruise on his back, and scratch on his knees—
Ze horses vare no vare!
Ze buggy turn ovare!
So he walk for five miles—in top boots and chemise?

A. Brodrick.

PRETORIA, 1882.

SOUTH AFRICAN COURTSHIP.

THE girl I love was bred and born
Close to the "winding" neck of Horn,*
 'Neath Cashan's purple splendour.

---

* Horn's Neck, Magaliesberg.

She is so fair, she is so good,
That, in her simple womanhood,
   You cannot mar or mend her.

You cannot mar her or improve—
Her voice is like the wild wood dove
   Cooing by river branches,
Her neck (unlike the neck of Horn)
Is white as Alpine snow down-borne
   By summer avalanches.

She is as graceful as the beech—
Her lips are ripe as blooming peach,
   Or like small twin tomatoes;
Her hair is black, her earrings jet,
Nature and art together met—
   For she to each a part owes.

Her teeth are white as sea-cow's tusk,
And gleam upon you in the dusk—
   Her eyes blue as seringa;
Her foot is shapely, and her hand,
And on her finger shines a band
   Of gold—her little finger!

I saw her standing on a chair
In a dark orange grove—aware,
   I fancy, of my presence;
For though she neither looked nor turned,
Her cheek with more than sunset burned,
   As if she felt Love's essence.

She raised herself upon her toes—
Regardless of her boots and hose
   (The day was one of March's),

She picked the fruit above her head,
And softly as a Zephyr said,
   "Mij oompie, hier is nartjes." *

I took the fruit, I took her hand—
I squeezed them both—you understand?
   I said, "Oh! let us wander
Beyond this darksome orange grove,
And talk of cattle—or of Love—
   My gentle Afrikander." †

I spoke to her in broken Dutch,
Or damaged English with a touch
   Of "Afrikander" in it.
I said to her—what did I say?
I said "ah! ja," I said "ah! nay,"
   And said so every minute.

I said "ah! ja, ik dank *u* veel," ‡
I'd thrown away the "nartje" peel
   And sucked the juices there-in;
I said "I love you," fruitful theme,
In such a case (I do not dream)
   A man becomes Man-darin.

She stood just then as once stood Ruth,
"Amid the alien corn"—in truth
   'Twas at no latticed casement—
'Twas in her father's "mealie" ground
I spoke—she started at the sound
   In mealies and a*maze*ment.

---

* "My uncle, here are small oranges" (or "Mandarin" oranges).
† Born in Africa of European parentage (originally).
‡ Ah! yes, I thank you much."

Oh! wonder not such things are done
So quickly 'neath a tropic sun—
  "There is no time to tarry"—
Love ripens faster than the pine,
The Lover says "Will you be mine?"
  Next week they go and marry.

I told her of my cows and calves,
And how with Thomson I was "halves,"
  And totted up the figures—
How waggons of my own, one, two,
Were earning much at Se-coo-coo-
  Ni's, fighting 'gainst the niggers.

I told her that I was an Earl
Disguised—she swallowed it, dear girl—
  I said I would repay her,
If she would give her heart to me,
A man used to society,
  A gentleman "Karreweijer." *

She said she'd cows and calves as well,
And oxen too, which she could sell—
  A "rustbank" † chair and poodle,
And breathing then a pensive sigh
She said, "some land too, by and by,
  A fourth of father's *boedel*." ‡

We sought her Pa—he smoking sat,
Beside him dogs upon a mat;
  He relished it, like butter—
He dropped his pipe and heaved a sigh,

---

* A "transport driver" or carrier.
† A home-made sofa. ‡ Estate.

> Then took a "tot"—then winked his eye
>   And said, "Neef jij kan vat haar."*
>
> So when I wed her, I shall "trek,"
> And go and live near Horn's long neck—
>   'Neath Cashan's regal splendour;
> Around her neck I'll place my arm,
> I'll get a quarter of the farm—
>   And throughout life defend her!

A. Brodrick.

PRETORIA, 1882.

THE BETTER LAND.

AFTER SHEMANS.

I HEAR thee speak of a better land,
Where farms are picked up, and the veld is grand;
Where game is plenty, and Natives weak,
And will work without giving us (gratis) cheek.
Father, oh! where is that home for the Boer?
Shall we not seek it and slave no more?
   We will, we will, my child!

Is it far away where the placid breast
Of N'Gami shines in "the purple west?"
Is it where Hermanus two years ago,
Found elephant, sea-cow, and buffalo?
Is it wooded or plain, inclined for flats?
Is it far, far north by old Selekats?
   Not there, not there, my child!

Is it past the Blueberg, and through the fly,
Where the men of Zoutpansberg used to die?

---

*_"Nephew, you can take her."

Is it north of Mapog or Sekookoon,
Where Mauch beheld Mrs. Sheba's "*Roon?*"
Near Origstadt or St. Lucia's Bay,
Where heaps of the bones of our fathers lay?
    Not there, not there, my child!

Is it on Zambesi, that mooi stream,
Where the veld's so thick that the cows' milk's cream,
Where the sun's so hot that all day we sleep—
Where Law and Government will be cheap?
Is it through the sand?—on the desert's hem?
Oom Piet—oh! is it Gee-roo-salem?
    Not there, not there, my child!

I have not seen it, my gentle neef,
It belongs to no regular King or Chief;
But far to the west, and near the sea,
Where the Damaras' dwell (spelt with capital "D.")
There is the land of our Hope—and Doom,
Far beyond Secheel, and beyond Sekoom.
    It is there, it is THERE, my child!

A. Brodrick.

PRETORIA, TRANSVAAL, 1879.

"DOLLY."

A REMEMBRANCE.

HERS was the voice that moved us when we woke,
In childish prattle, or in broken song,
Hers was the smile, that like a sunbeam broke
Through all our clouds, and shone all cares among.

And now, like dearest things of priceless cost,
We only feel her value, when she's lost.

So small, so young, and yet she made a place
We ne'er can fill, which never can be filled;
Where e'er we turn, we still can see her face,
And in the silent night our hearts are thrilled
By her small voice, as if what was our own
Feared yet to leave us, and to be alone.

We only understand our bitter loss,
But not the little life so filled with pain,
We cannot understand the heavy cross
Borne by our darling flower without a stain :
We only know a grace has from us passed,
And a dark cloud upon our lives is cast.

Her little playmates stood with awe and love
Around her grave, and sang the while she slept;
But when the bright blue sky was hidden above,
They stood in silence, and in silence wept;
They knew her little feet would never tread
Again this earth, which covered her fair head.

Farewell, dear child! We still shall touch thy hand,
We still shall see thy face, and hear thy tongue.
Where art thou? In the far-off heavenly land,
With Christ's protecting love around thee thrown?
Where art thou? Shall we meet thee ne'er to part,
And know thee as of old—Light of our heart?

A. Brodrick.

PRETORIA, *November* 17, 1874.

GOING HOME.

FROM THE TRANSVAAL TO ENGLAND.

Why are we going? Joking apart—
To wake our soul, and lift our heart,
To wear the crust from the mildewed brain,
And stand in the ranks of the world again.
To see, hear, feel, each beauteous thing;
That civilisation alone can bring;
To walk 'neath roofs that knew the flow
Of music, centuries ago;
To stand in temples where have trod,
For ages, worshippers of God;
To stand by marts where Argosies
At anchor lie, from distant seas,
Ships that say: "all *'neath* the sun
By ties of nature are made one;"
Ships that tell with their white wings furled
How throbs *with one great pulse the world!*

Why are we going? To see, though men,
The Home where we lived as boys, again;
To see *her* face in its sunset glow,
That lighted the Home of our *Long ago*,
To feel our rough rind fall away,
And our hearts receive the light of day.
Let us drop the pen, and the lightsome word,
And think of that dear old Home. How stirred
Are memories as we sit and sigh,
And the years on lightning feet flit by,
And the patient Love, the watchful care,
Rise out of the distant landscape fair,

And a word of deepest love will rise
For her, who now longs with tear-filled eyes
To welcome the way-worn wand'rer *home*,
Just as of old her boy will come!
No change in the love, that bore all ills,
As eternal as God's own grassy hills.

A. Brodrick.

Pretoria, 1879.

THE OXFORD BIBLE.

ON WORN-OUT SAILS BEING USED AS MATERIAL FOR THE MANUFACTURE OF PAPER ON WHICH BIBLES ARE PRINTED.

The breezes free of the great white sea
   Have filled us with strength and life;
And the ocean gales have driven our sails
   In the midst of the billows' strife.

To the South from North have we oft gone forth
   To sail o'er the bright sunny seas;
We've been kissed by an air most pure and fair,
   And been lulled by the evening breeze.

Full many a time, in a tropic clime,
   We've been wooed by the sun's hot breath,
And mid frozen hail we have felt the flail
   Of the Lord of the Ice and Death.

Under stormy skies, amid Nature's cries,
   We have struggled and fought for life,
And then wearied and worn with work well borne,
   We have finished our early strife.

Our labours had ceased, and we were released
   From the sun and the winds and the gales,

Our voyages passed, we sank down at last
   As old, tattered, and worn-out sails.

But we now rise again with glad refrain,
   We rise in a book of peace,
Amid hymn and psalm, and words of balm,
   And a message which ne'er shall cease.

And risen we find our sea is the mind,
   Our voyage is fair and free;
Through brain and through soul, we pass to the goal
   Of God and Eternity.

Marie.

THE LAST MISSION OF THE SAILS.

The sails of the ships are lying,
   White on the floor of the mill,
Scarr'd with the wounds of the weather,
   But sweet with the sea scent still.
Fresh from the spray of the sunshine,
   And braving the tempest's rage,
To the whirr and the hum of the wheels they come,
   And the calm of the printed page.

Aloft from the spreading yard-arms,
   They bent o'er the distant seas,
To the blast of the frozen Horn
   Or sigh of the tropic breeze.
A message of might is tokened
   On the cloths of each tattered sail,
For they bear the brand of the Storm King's hand
   In the strain of the sea and gale.

In a fairer form, and purer,
  They come from the mill at last,
Transformed, as man hereafter,
  When the wondrous change is past.
Between the boards of the Bible
  The sails of the ships shall rest,
While they speed again o'er the troubled main
  With the Master's Word impressed.

Adamastor.

THE WORN-OUT SAILS.

Take down the sails, the worn and ragged sails,
  Let them no longer flutter in the breeze,
And bear the gallant vessels to and fro
  Over the seas, the blue and smiling seas.

They are so old, and worn, and tattered now,
  Their work is done—shall they be cast away
As worthless rubbish, only fit to lie
  And moulder in the dust-heaps, to decay?

No; put them to a greater, nobler use,
  Give them a better purpose than before,
When the sun shone upon them white and new,
  And when from shore to shore the ships they bore.

Wash all their dust, and stains, and spots away,
  And fashion from them paper pure and fair,
And then when this thou hast completed, in
  The leaves let God's own blessed word appear.

Let the glad message of the Gospel shine
  Upon the unsullied whiteness of each page,

The gentle words our blessèd Saviour spoke,
  And the grand thoughts of prophets old and sage.

The worn-out sails, great service they have done,
  We will not let them perish and decay,
This, their last work, the greatest and the best,
  It shall preserve them in our land for aye.

The stately ships that sail the ocean wide,
  Can England guard from foe and hostile band;
But God's word in the people's hearts, is still
  The secret of the greatness of our land.

E. L. B. (*Alice*).

IN MEMORIAM.

GORDON is dead: and lo! the unconscious wire
  Carries the mournful message on its way,
Girdling the globe with news of direst truth,
  From Egypt's minarets to broad Cathay.

The Christian soldier, and the Christian man,
  Sleeps by the side of Nile's historic wave,
Rescued by Death, his freedom is secured,
  And now he wears the garments of the brave.

In vain the stubborn fight of Abu Klea;
  In vain Metammeh's more than brilliant charge;
Gordon is dead; England is craped in black,
  And funeral echoes pall the world at large.

'Twas treachery that struck the fatal blow;
  Traitors within the walls of far Khartoum,
Laid the invincible for ever low,
  And sealed their own irrevocable doom.

Vengeance is sometimes slow but always sure,
  The might of England rushes to the fray,
Even now the Mahdi's reign is almost o'er;
  Vengeance is England's, and she will repay.

Forward, Sir Garnet! even here our eyes
  And ears are strained for victory's sights and sounds;
We wait for tidings, for indeed we know
  In British armour bravery still abounds.

Forward! and soon the victory shall be yours,
  Avenge the slaughtered dead about Khartoum,
Nail to the colours England's last commands,
  Stern and sincere, "Room for Sir Garnet, room!"

Forward; and drive the Arab hordes beyond
  The reach of Nile's exhilarating flood,
And teach fanaticism what it means
  To traffic heedlessly in Christian blood.

Garret Brown.

EPITAPH ON A DIAMOND DIGGER.

Here lies a digger, all his chips departed—
A splint of nature, bright, and ne'er down-hearted:
He worked in many claims, but now (though stumped)
He's got a claim above that can't be jumped.
May he turn out a pure and spotless "wight,"
When the Great Judge shall sift the wrong from right,
And may his soul, released from this low Babel,
Be found a gem on God's great sorting table.

A. Brodrick.

KIMBERLEY, 1875.

AFRIC'S GREETING

TO HER ROYAL HIGHNESS ALEXANDRA, PRINCESS OF WALES, ON HER WEDDING DAY, MARCH 10, 1863.

Royal Lady! O'er the ocean
   Afric's greeting speeds to thee!
Borne on sighs of fond emotion;
   Full of loyal, true devotion;
Honest, candid, open, free,
   Just what Britons' love should be.
Fresh from every heart and hand;
   Warm as is our sunny land;
Hopeful as the future life
Must be, of our Albert's wife;
Full of frank and honest pride,
As thy husband at thy side
Must be, owning thee as bride.
   Lady! o'er Britannia's sea
   Afric's greeting speeds to thee!

Lady! though we are not near thee—
   Far by wave and storm exiled:—
Twofold is the love we bear thee—
   Love of parent and of child.
Parent's love, for thy youth still hath
   Claim to parent's anxious care;
Child's love, for when Heaven willeth
   Thou that honoured throne must share;
Then, as now, our hearts will greet thee,
   Though *far distant be the day;*
For we love our peerless Sov'reign
   And would keep her while we **may**.

That pure reign which comes before thee,
  Crowned by virtues erst unknown,
Teaches thee a golden secret
  Ne'er before to monarchs known.
Teaches thee the golden secret,
  Won by virtue from above,
HOW TO RULE A LOYAL PEOPLE
  AND RETAIN THEIR FERVENT LOVE.
Imitate it! Emulate it!
  Thus our hopes of thee fulfil;—
Thus thy great and loyal people
  Will be great and loyal still.
Thus, dear lady, o'er the sea
Afric hopes and prays for thee!

H. W. Bidwell.

GRAHAMSTOWN, *May* 1863.

ROBERT GODLINTON.

Born in London, September 1794; died at Grahamstown,
30th May 1884.

MOURN, Africa! your oldest, noblest sage
  Sleeps the long sleep. Your noblest? Aye! for he
  Whose name the roll of true nobility
Next heads, may well be proud. How bright a page
His history fills. The *Franklin* of our age,
  Who wrought for Truth, for Liberty, and Light.
The aim of all his fourscore years and ten
Was "Peace on earth and good will towards men;"
  Right for the wrongèd weak—for wronging right
Confusion. How he strove with sword, tongue, pen,

Q

  As soldier, statesman, writer! giving all
The glorious dower of his heart and brain
To us and God: until He took again
  The life, which could we, we would fain recall.
The measure of his influence who can tell?—
  We know not whether from that distant home
  To which th' All-Wise has ta'en him, he may come
In spirit to the land he served so well.
  But this we know :—The good that he has wrought,
  Th' examples set, the lessons he has taught,
As scattered seed on Time's e'er-rolling flood
Immortal are, and can but work us good.

H. W. Bidwell.

THE DIAMOND DIGGER.

ON FINDING HIS FIRST LARGE DIAMOND.

(From the drama "I. D. B.")

WHAT change of luck! O Fortune! they have well
Compared thee to a woman ;—ever flying,
But luring on, when Hope-led we pursue ;—
And when we scorn thee, coming back, all smiles,
O'erwhelming us with richest, choicest favours.
(*Looks at the diamond.*) Can it be real?—Can I believe
  my eyes?
A gem like thee would grace a monarch's crown ;
Aye! and would buy his empire from him too.
For smaller and less precious gems than thee
Have monarchs been betrayed and empires sold.
For less than thee, Beauties, whose hearts of steel
Not all the worship of true love could move,
Have given their charms to arms they else had loathed.

But oh! thou glittering bauble! Canst thou buy
One sigh of pure affection! one small grain
Of Truth?—Call back the loved ones gone?
Give respite to the wretch condemned to die?
Or win redemption for a soul that's lost?
Ah, no! Truth is the bright, pure gem!
Compared with her thou'rt very dross indeed.
Yet thou art mine! mine! mine! my own!
Mine only! And as yet no other eyes
But mine have gazed upon thy dazzling splendour.
How strange it seems that thou who hast lain hid
Down in the very heart of Earth; and in
The very womb, as 'twere, of hoary Time,
Cycles long, long ere History was born,
Now comest forth, like some new-chos'n Sultana
From the zenana's gloom, where all her light,
Her glory, and her beauty, blazed in vain!
The fabled Sleeping Beauty sure thou wert!
I the proud Prince whose vivifying touch
Called thee to light and gave thy splendour life;—
The thought is overpowering; and the feeling
With which I call thee mine is not all joy.
I've heard how gems like thee, which it has cost
The owners years of patient toil to win,
Have caused their death when won;—that woe, not bliss,
Have followed their possession; and a thrill
While now I clutch thee seemeth to forebode
Some coming evil. Were it known I go
About with a king's ransom in my pocket,
My life would not be safe. No! I must hide
Thee as a thief would hide his stolen prize.

H. W. Bidwell.

THE LAST OF THE BOWKERS.

A DIRGE.

A<small>LAS</small>! Is it true that the great R. M. Bowker
  No longer in Parliament covets a place?
But follows his brethren—this gigantic joker?
  The greatest—the last of a very slow race.

First Thomas the tartar; then William the wailer,
  Knocked under; they couldn't keep pace with the age.
Now the last of the trio, great Robert the *railer*,
  Has made his *Bow cur*tly and gone from the stage.

But oh! in the Senate the *gap* will be shocking!
  Long, long will be missed that cantankerous face—
He stood six feet three in his veldschoen and stocking.
  'Twill take a braw chiel, mon, to *fill up* his place.

Though his broadcloth was broadest, his humour was
      broader—
  Though his legs were the longest, the length of his jaw
Out-did them; yet he was ne'er once called to order,
  By the fierce little knight whose mere wig's nod was
      law.*

There may in the future be low jokes and high jokes;
  And good jokes and jokes good for nothing at all—
But no more his sly jokes, his wry jokes and dry jokes—
  For this *flower* of all jokers is gone to the *wall*.

But oh! on the road, as life's journey we drag on,
  Whether main road or branch, Grief will turn on *her*
      main,

---

* Speaker Brand.

To think how that highly distinguished buck wagon
  Will ne'er take that *buck* of a *wag on* again.
Yet, a paradox, trekking along on the mail road,
  He was, as I'll prove, though 'twill nothing avail.
Though he growled at the railroad and kept the old frail
    road,
  The whole of his journey he kept *on the rail*.

But what of the "House" without one Bowker in it?
  Like a waggon deprived of its break, down 'twill go,
And the whole span of Parliament into infinite
  Disorder will rush, with their *Achter os flauw*.

Well, peace to the *manes* of these shaggy old lions!
  May the song of the steam-engine lull them to rest;
May they, free from "obstruction," "protest," and
    "defiance"
  (But not in a buck-waggon) go to the blest.

Be this their escutcheon :—A steam-engine rampant,
  A patriot floored on the floor of the "House,"
A skinned nigger salient—sixteen oxen couchant,
  A waggon smashed up, and a broken-down smouse.

H. W. Bidwell.

UITENHAGE, *May* 21.

THE DRUNKARD'S CHILD.

FOUNDED ON ONE OF J. B. GOUGH'S THRILLING ANECDOTES.

" I CANNOT spare that book, papa—
  Take all I have beside;
But that my poor, my dear mamma,
  Gave me the day she died,

"And bade me keep it for her sake;—
   If all your money's spent
Sell all my toys, but do not take
   My little Testament!

"She told me that I there might read
   The way to heaven above.
I cannot part with it indeed!—
   Her last dear gift of love."

There stood beside that couch of straw,
   All haggard, wretched, wild,
The drunkard father, staggering o'er
   His sweet but dying child.

And as she spoke, a father's tear
   Stole down his bloated cheek;
And thus he cried, "Hush, Fanny dear!
   'Tis not your book I seek.

"But oh! this cursed, burning thirst,
   Has made me mad, I think;
I take your book!—I'd perish first—
   And yet I must have drink!—

"Come, child! no more that sad pale look!—
   There—dry your weeping eye,
I would not steal your little book
   For all the world—not I!"

Her sighs and sobs are now at rest,
   For see! the maiden sleeps;—
But closely to her little book,
   The Testament, she keeps.

There bathed in beauteous tears she lay,
   Like some half drooping flower,
Cropt ere the sun had kissed away
   The grief of evening's hour.

There stood the man; his burning tongue
   Half cursing his intent,
As stealthily from Fanny's breast
   He took the Testament.

Not all a father's love could break
   The dread, the cursed spell
That binds the drunkard to his glass,
   And drags his soul to hell.

But deaf to sweet affection's voice,
   Dead to the fear of sin,
Away he bore the cherished pledge
   And bartered it for gin.

Now once again he dares beside
   That wretched couch to stand;
And gazes on his dying child
   The bottle in his hand.—

How shall he meet her dying face?
   He dare not, cannot think,
But all reflection, all disgrace
   Drowns in absorbing drink,—

But see! his little daughter wakes,
   And seeks her book in vain,
Yet murmurs not—how calm she takes
   The sickness and the pain.

But though the ghastly hues of death
    O'er her wan features roll,
A beam of immortality
    Is borrowed from the soul,

That lightens up her waning eye
    With an unearthly light,
That tells the spirit plumes its wings
    For an eternal flight.

" Father," she cried, " I'm dying now;
    Nay, father ! do not weep !—
I know you took my Testament
    When I was fast asleep.

" But I forgive you, father dear !
    Come !—sit down by my side !—
Say ! do you think I'll get to heaven ?
    You know how hard I've tried.

" I think I shall—I know I shall—
    For in my book I read
' *Let little children come to Me,*'
    That's what the Saviour said.

" But, father, when I get to heaven
    And my poor dear mamma,
And all those angels pure and bright
    Shall speak of you, papa !

" And ask me what you did with it,
    My mother's darling book—
What shall your Fanny say to them ?—
    Father !—how ill you look ! "—

" Oh ! mercy, child ! " the father cries,
    " What hope is there for me,

Oh! I have broken all the ties
   Of loved humanity!—

"See here!" and with a dreadful oath
   The bottle down he cast—
"Thus do I break the drunkard's chains
   —I've freed myself at last."

"Nay! curse not, father dear, but pray."—
   "How can I pray," he cried.
"I'll teach you, father; come this way!—
   There—kneel down by my side!"—

He knelt, and in response to her,
   Repeated word for word—
"*To me a sinner deep and black*
   Be merciful, O Lord!"

She died—and as the angels bore
   Her little spirit home,
They sang in joy o'er the drunkard's soul
   Thus rescued from its doom.*

H. W. Bidwell.

THE ANGEL'S MESSAGE.

'Twas a beautiful evening:—towards the calm west
   The god of the summer triumphantly rolled;
As the glory gates oped to receive their bright guest
   They let out a torrent of heaven's own gold.

---

* I publish this piece at the request of several friends, but cannot suffer it to go forth with all its imperfections, without putting forward as an apology for them the fact that it was written when the author was very young, and ignorant of the rules of composition.

It mellowed the lawn, where the poplar's tall spire
   Threw a shade, which dissolved as it longer became.
It lit up the hall like a temple of fire
   As its old Norman windows reflected the flame.

All was silent; for Philomel yet did not raise
   His song, which both sadness and rapture inspire:
The thrush and finch ceased their vesper of praise
   To gaze on the glory and mutely admire.

The newly born zephyr, so gentle and mild,
   Strayed over the lawn to a chamber above,
Where her sad mother sighed o'er her withering child,
   The frail blossom born of unsanctified love.

Oh! the sigh from an innocent heart—like the breeze
   Which distils from the flowers those essences rare,
Too subtle for e'en the inquisitive bees—
   Is laden with sweetness that medicines care.

But not so the breathings exhaled from the breast
   Where guilt makes a sepulchre, shame finds a home;
And the hope that with virtue alone deigns to rest,
   With its heavenly solace may never more come.

Yet the scene was so tranquil, the grandeur so calm,
   That its influence e'en to that sad heart would steal;
Like an angel of charity pouring its balm
   To soothe the deep wound that it never might heal.

And the mother sat watching that dear life, whose ebb
   Was so stealthy, that even love's fears were beguiled,
Till the spider-fay sleep spun its magical web
   'Twixt the frail one's fond eyes and her innocent child.

And the soft zephyrs played on each delicate brow,
  Like tender caresses of angels unseen;
Now lifting a curl from a forehead of snow,
  Now kissing a cheek where a tear-pearl had been.

They are dreaming—Hark!—Whence that mysterious sound?
  Like the wild harp of Æolus disturbed by the wings
Of some spirit that playfully hovers around,
  And fan into song the invisible strings;

Or the hymn which the spirit of God's universe
  Sings unto the planets and suns, as they roll,
Or the chorus celestial beings rehearse
  When they welcome to heaven an innocent soul.

Lo! a ladder of sunbeams shoots down from the skies
  To the child, and a host of bright beings appear;
And as they descend their sweet voices arise
  More loud and distinct on the mother's rapt ear.

Oh! ne'er has the tongue of a mortal expressed
  The accents that fall on the ears of the soul,
The thoughts to an atom of spirit addressed
  By its infinite, mighty, mysterious whole.

The silver-winged choristers press round the pair;
  The chorus has ceased; but a voice far more sweet
In its unaided melody, takes up the air,
  Which feebly the muse thus essays to repeat.

"This is the dear sister our love longs to win,
  Soft!—bear her away to the home of the blest,
Ere a pang of earth's sorrow, or taint of its sin,
  Hath stricken or sullied her innocent breast."

They raise her; again in rich harmony blend
  The sweet voices; a glance half of joy, half of pain
They beam on the mother, then gracefully wend
  Their ethereal pathway to heaven again.

The chorus expires:—their images shown
  In the dimness of distance like faint shadows seem;
Till the gates now regained are wide open thrown,
  And each form stands revealed in the outrushing gleam.

The child is upraised in a halo of light
  More radiant far than was e'er seen on this earth;
It smiles an adieu!—then departs from the sight;
  The gates close:—it enters its heavenly birth!

All was dark till a bright star appeared in the place,
  Shedding down like a beacon of hope its pure ray,
And the mother awaking, rushed forth to embrace—
  Not her child—but the husk which its soul cast away.

And oft, when the earliest shadows of night
  Veil the earth, the bereaved one will gaze on that star;
There is joy in its glory and hope in its light,
  For it seems like her child looking down from afar.

H. W. Bidwell.

GRAHAMSTOWN, 1862.

THE "CHURL" OF THE PERIOD; AND ANOTHER.

A LEGEND OF THE PAST, PRESENT, AND FUTURE.

THE CHURL.

WILD, wild was the night on the wild, wild karoo—
Confoundedly wild near the kraal called "Barroo"

(Although after Kirkwood's advertisement readin',
You'd think "Barroo Kraal" Hottentot-Dutch for Eden);
Well, the storm monarch *reigned* in this wild wilderness,
And a trav'ler who *hailed* from the port Little Bess,
Reined his charger and then through the darkness did peer,
Twigged some *lights* and concluded a *liver* was near;
For he *longed* that he *shortly* some shelter might find,
Did this travel-worn *Reed shaken* by the wild *wind*.
The *lightning* was blazing behind and before,
So he *thundered* away at the house of the Boer.

In a *crack* and his *crackers*, mynheer did appear,
And exclaimed, "In de naam van de drommel, wie's daar?"
Said the stranger, "I'm shaking from toe-tip to crown,
These roads *shake* me up, so I crave a *shake-down!*
Barroo Kraal's some distance,—my steed is so weary,
He'd *ne'er crawl* to *carry* me *near* to friend *Cary*.
I don't *care-a-button* how poor is your cheer,
But in mercy I pray you to put me somewhere."
Mynheer gave a grunt, and he slammed to the door,
And our friend was "left out in the cold" as before.

Three months had passed by when quite early one day
This *intractable* Boer made *tracks* to the Bay.
He was met by our friend, who had now ceased to roam,
And kindly invited to go with him home.
So he went with our friend and entered his house,
And was thus introduced to his genial spouse.
"I've brought *home* a queer kind of *homo*, my dear,
Let not *home-opathy* curtail your cheer,

Get best things in season, in order to show
Hospitality's here as well's up by Barroo!"

The table soon groaned 'neath the daintiest store
That ever yet tickled the taste of a Boer—
Mynheer guzzled coffee with Hennessy's "stick" in,
And stowed away no end of broiled ham and chicken;
The crevices filling up well with poached eggs,
Till, tight as a drum, he arose on his legs—
His host arose also—and cried, "You old beast!
You've sat at my table and gorged at my feast!
And you're welcome. You taught me some three months
    ago
How *you* receive trav'lers who can't reach 'Barroo;'
I've returned you the compliment, old boy, to-day,
For I've shown you how guests are received at the Bay—
Lest the lesson be lost on so churlish a lout,
Take that, sir!—and that!" and he kicked him bang out.

ANOTHER.

A Governor felt it his duty to go
To arrange matters 'twixt one King John and his foe,
Between whom had arisen bloodthirsty dissensions,
But t'wards this Boer King he'd the kindest intentions.
John couldn't have treated him worse had he been
The agent of Moshesh instead of the Queen.
Not a single gun popped off a sensation louder—
(Perhaps that's because he was hard up for powder)—
But, for all that was done by this potentate bold,
Sir Philip too might have stopped "out in the cold,"
For the welcome John gave him a name comes in handy,
The *spirit* he showed to his guest was *Boer-Brandy*.

Three months had passed by, and King John, now at peace,
From work and for office obtained a *re-lease;*
So primed well with blue-blacks he thought he'd go down
To spend *them* and his holidays there in Cape Town.
When the Governor heard John was coming that way,
He said, "'Tis my turn at 'reception' to play.
Let those guns which since Duke Alfred came have been mute
Be *charged* to *discharge* him a royal salute,
Cripps! *lion* King John, like a real *kingly brute;*
And soldiers! be sure you do the right thing,
Let an *orderly* tend this *disorderly* king!
Get rolls of tobacco his pipe well to cram,
And lay in a stock of Cape smoke and schiedam,
And order some horse hides, first hand, from our knacker's,
To make him a pair of right regal Boer crackers—
He'll go to bed in them, but that doesn't matter;
Put him up in my bed, 'twill his vanity flatter,
I can sleep on the sofa or hearthrug instead—
We must heap coals of fire on King Johnny's head.
He has shown me how *friends* are received in the *Free*
State; I'll show him how *foes* are received here by me.

MORAL.

'Twill be strange now if all this "reception" and rout
Should end in John's getting the "dirty kick out."

W. H. Bidwell.

UITENHAGE, 24*th June* 1869.

WELCOME.

LET gladness fill our British homes,
All hearts rejoice! a victor comes:—
Not like the conquerors of yore
With laurels stained by human gore.
Let earth a floral welcome yield,
No devastation marks the field
Whereon his victory was gained,
His triumph's peaceful and unstained.

Let little children's voices rise,
For no discordant orphans cries
Shall mar their glee. His deeds, though great,
And pregnant with the will of fate,
Are heralds of a happier day,
And pure and innocent as they.

Let gentle ladies lend their cheers,
His conquest's free from widow's tears;
Let manly voices swell the strain,
His course is not o'er brother's slain;
No soldiers scarred and maimed proclaim
A bloody source of all his fame.
His triumph is o'er ancient wrong,
O'er prejudices old and strong,
'Time honoured; time dishonouring—
Peace, Justice, Hope, 'tis his to bring.

Children of loyal men! 'tis meet
Your cherub voices fresh and sweet
Should rise to heaven in welcome cheers;
For when in your maturer years
The seed 'tis his blest work to sow
Shall spring up round you—with you grow,

And cover like some sheltering tree
Your future, happier destiny.
Your voices then much deeper grown,
Shall tell to children, then your own,
How Wodehouse and his noble dame
'Midst shouts of infant welcome came;
How ranged like soldiers on the green
You sang " GOD SAVE OUR GRACIOUS QUEEN."

He comes like meteor bright and bold,
Scorning the track traversed of old
By orbs whose fastly waning light
Is sinking in the realms of night.
He seeks the cradle of the dawn,
Where Freedom's sun proclaims the morn—
This day we'll give to joy at least;
This day the light dawns in the East,
And soon beneath its genial ray
North, South, East, West, shall feel 'tis day.

H. W. Bidwell.

GRAHAMSTOWN, *Feb.* 1, 1864.

PRECEPTS FOR YOUNG AND OLD.

I'D like to speak a word to you, my pretty, careless child!
I'd learn the spell that daily lures you 'midst the blossoms wild,
I'd join you and the butterflies with which you sport and play,
As innocent, as beautiful, as fairy-like as they.
I'd like to scan the purity that halos your fair brow,
To fathom all the gentle thoughts that through your bosom flow—

But oh! the wish is doubly vain, 'tis not for heart like mine
To enter that pure heaven which forms the fairy land of thine.

I'd like to speak a word with you, my timid blushing maid—
Pausing at every step you take as if you were afraid!
As if by instinct you foresaw the weeds of woe and strife,
That grow up in the pathway of your unseen future life.
Oh! happy, ten times happy, were you could you shun the wild
And rugged waste; and turning back for ever, be a child.
You cannot! then I'd say to you, retain as best you may
The pure and holy freshness of your childhood's cloudless day!

I'd like to speak a word with you, my bold and wayward youth!
I'd counsel you to cherish in your heart the love of truth;
I'd caution you 'gainst wantonness and arrogance and pride,
And bid you fear your passions more than all the world beside.
I'd have you honour age whose precepts now you hear with scorn,
Remember! we were men, my boy, long, long ere you were born,
Have trodden long ago the path which you have yet to tread,
And now bequeath experience which may serve you when we're dead.

I'd like to speak a word with you, brave sir, in manhood's prime!
The world seems now your heritage, and 'tis so—for a time.
Aspire! for 'tis your birthright, but remember while you mount
You're but a steward and some day must yield up your account.
You're wealthy!—turn not from the poor!. they share your right to live,
Or God would not have made them :—as you've received, so give;
Nor like the unjust creditor, seize all man's laws allow,
You will need mercy at the last, see that you mete it now!

I'd speak to you, grey-headed man! now tottering at death's door,
Gazing on life's red page, by sin and sorrow blotted o'er.
How wistfully you eye that past you never may recall,
And wish, since life must end like this, you'd never lived at all.
Oh! look to Him whom you despised, while 'twas your lot to live;
Remember! mercy is His will; His first wish to forgive.
Haste! for that dark door opens! be saved while yet you may!
Alas! that it should close again, and you should pass away.

H. W. Bidwell.

GRAHAMSTOWN, *October* 1, 1863.

BE KIND TO ONE ANOTHER.

Be kind to one another!
    Th' alchemist's magic stone
That turns to gold the dross of life,
    Is love and love alone.
How many who now fret and weep
    All minor griefs might smother,
If they would but this mandate keep,—
    " Be kind to one another."

Be kind to one another!
    Sweet words and gentle looks
Set free the love-streams of the soul,
    As springs unlock the brooks;
But pride and coldness seal the hearts
    Of good men from each other.
If thou wouldst learn men's nobler parts
    Be kind to one another!—

Be kind to one another!
    What though a churlish elf
Thy neighbour seem! Must thou retort,
    And be as bad thyself?
Couldst thou the secret heart behold
    Of any erring brother,
Thou in the worst wouldst find some gold—
    Be kind to one another.

Be kind to one another!
    Life is too short to waste
In foolish enmity and strife,—
    Time flies with ruthless haste;—

Soon death with an impartial hand
    Will level foe and brother,
Oh! prize the hours thou mayst command—
    Be kind to one another!

H. W. Bidwell.

PADDY'S LOVE SYMPTOMS.

FOR MUSIC.

Oh! what have you done wid me, Daisy?
    You plump little rosy young witch!
Sure my head and my heart's so unaisy
    I scarcely can tell which is which.
Whene'er I come in your sweet presence
    It's telegraphed all o'er I feel;
If I touch you, och! murther! it kills me
    Jest like an electrified eel.

Your eyes are like flashings of lightning,
    Glancing there, darting here, oh! so frisky;
Your sweet breath's more intoxicating
    By far than old Irish whisky!
Each eye, each limb, and each action,
    Your garments, too, every stitch
Are all bent on Patrick's destruction,
    You plump little rosy young witch!

I learned a long speech to say to you
    When I came to your house t'other day,
But I sat there as dumb as mackerel,
    And that's every word I could say.

For my heart grew so awfully jealous
  To think that my tongue should address you,
That it jumped up and stuck in my throttle
  Before I could gasp out " God bless you."

I told the good father confessor
  My troubles, says he, " Pat ! I'm sure
You're bewitched by some wicked young fairy,
  And I only know one means of cure ! "
But he says that same cure is quite aisy,
  He'll soon make all right, if I bring
To church, one fine morn, my sweet Daisy,
  And likewise a little gold ring.

H. W. Bidwell.

PROVERBIAL PHILOSOPHY OF HUMBUG.

GREAT is the power of Humbug. Credulous, very, is Bunkum,—

Bunkum that seeth things only as they are distorted by Humbug,—

Humbug that useth poor Bunkum's vanity, whims, and caprices

As medicines through which to show him the facts and the figures around him.

Facts are reputed as stubborn; but not half so stubborn as asses,

Asses who spurn out at facts and bray at the mention of figures,

Figures that show that the West is the spot that aboundeth in asses.

Great is the power of Humbug, credulous very are asses;

Hast thou not heard of a quadruped, of this same genus
—Jerusalem—
Innocent slave of a needy but very ingenious carpenter?
Carpenter, who the green spectacles fixed on the nose of his neddy,—
Neddy, who straightway ate shavings, thinking them first-rate green forage?
That was the triumph of Humbug over the weakness of Bunkum.
Even thus Bunkum devoureth the rubbish presented by Humbug.
True that the simile's wooden; true that the metaphor's donkeyfied!
Asinine also and wooden the subject it seeketh to illustrate.
Solomon's famed for his wisdom,—Molteno's Solomon's prophet—
Small is the profit that Solomon's wisdom secureth his minions;
He putteth green spectacles fast on the nose of poor Western neddies,—
The poor mokes believe his chaff grass, and devour it all with much gusto.
Figures are all topsy-turvable; may be read backwards or forwards;
Sixes inverted are nines, and nines with their tails off are ciphers,—
All Western donkeys are curtailed, thus *there* is *no end* of asses.
Dobson went forth from the East with his cranium crammed full of figures,
Figures which made the inflated Westerns to let off their gas

And collapse like mere bubbles of error when pierced by the arrows of truth.
Dobson retired from the conquest to rest 'neath the shade of his laurels,
Molteno purloined his figures and curtailed his nines and his sixes;
And all this to show that the rotten old shank bone abounded in maggots.
Dobson returned unsuspecting, to visit the scene of past glory,—
Oh! how the poor neddies brayed when they fancied the trick had succeeded,
Oh! what an asinine chorus greeted the hero's returning!
What wonder that Dobson retreated disgusted, nauseated, and bilious?
The stomach, accustomed to good Christian beef and orthodox cabbage,
Will turn against infidel snork, and rice is its abomination.
Disgust they mistook for defeat, contempt they imagined was chagrin,—
What bad living did for our hero, they fancied their wit had accomplished.
Contempt and disgust are too dignified weapons for poor abject Bunkum,
Still they bray o'er their own self-deception—while Dobson sits calm in his garden
Smoking his dudeen, the calumet of a sound head and clear conscience,—
He knows, though his figures were stolen and mischievously mutilated,
Like the sheep of Bo-peep they'll come home and bring all their pendants behind.

H. W. Bidwell.

July 28, 1865.

PLATTEKLIP CASCADE.

WHERE th' Olympian cloth is spread,
There thou'rt cradled, nursed, and bred;
  Bursting into life anew,
  Thirsting for celestial dew;
Drinking from th' ambrosial fountain,
Sinking through the veinèd mountain;
     Moving;
     Roving;
       Gravitating;
     Sliding;
     Gliding;
       Percolating;
Coursing on through channels hidden,
Forcing passages unbidden;
  Winding into cave and cell,
  Finding out where Naiads dwell;
Spirting out through crack and chink,
Flirting on each flower-clad brink;
  Creeping over banks and bosses,
  Weeping with the moist-eyed mosses;
Straying on midst foliage fair,
Playing with sweet maiden hair;
  Rippling through enchanted grots;
  Tippling with forget-me-nots,
Swelling into pools translucent,
Welling over, wild, recusant!
     Dashing;
       Flushing;
     Splashing;
       Gushing;

Whirling;
 Eddying;
Swirling;
 Rushing;
Spreading out upon the plain,
Threading on thy course again;
 Flowing brook-like through the wood,
 Growing to a larger flood;
Fertilising, fructifying,
Man's and Nature's needs supplying;
 Gliding down time's silent river;
To the ocean of For Ever.

B.

THE PORT ELIZABETH PYRAMID.

The Pyramid which forms the subject of the following lines is the most prominent historical monument of Port Elizabeth. It stands on the brow of the hill overlooking Algoa Bay, in an open space known as the "Donkin Reserve." It is built of rough stone and is about 35 feet in height, each side of the base being about 25 feet. On its western side a slate tablet is inserted exhibiting the following inscription :—

"Elizabeth Frances, Lady Donkin, eldest daughter of Dr. George Markham, Dean of York, died at Merat, in Upper Hindostan, of a fever, after seven days' illness, on the 21st August 1818, aged not quite 28 years. She left an infant in his seventh month, too young to know the unequalled loss he had sustained, and a husband whose heart is still wrung by undimished grief. He erected this Pyramid, August 1820."

On its eastern side a similar tablet appears exhibiting the following :—

"To the memory of one of the most perfect of human beings, who has given her name to the town below."

"Sermons in stones, and good in everything."—SHAKESPEARE.

I SEEK not with a weak and untuned lyre
To sound the praise of Cheop's mighty pile,
Where toiling myriads, higher and still higher,
In the dim past, beside the swirling Nile,

Heaped up those giant masses to the sky,
Upon whose hoary sides old Time's grim teeth
Have spent their force in vain.   From task so high
My muse with trembling shrinks.   If e'er a wreath
Should decorate her brow, 'twill twine 'mong themes
Of lowly sort.   Be hers the touch that thrills
Heart's deepest chords.   Be hers the light that beams
From Nature's restful face,—the love that fills
The Home with flowers of Eden's chastened bloom.
And surely this love-reared memorial pile
To sacred dust enshrined in Indian Tomb
A theme congenial yields.   The worldling's smile,
Incredulous, mayhap reveals the thought
That from rough stone no poet flowers can rise
In gladd'ning bloom, no wisdom's lore be taught.
    Erected here perchance to tranquillise
That "undiminished grief" whose darksome tide
For two long years had whelmed Sir Rufane's heart,
This Pyramid on Donkin's Hill beside
The tow'ring light-house stands;· and with rude art
Its sculptured tablets tell that she whose loss
The stricken husband mourned, a babe had left
Too young to feel the orphan's bitter cross;
And earth in her recall had been bereft
Of one pure gem whose ray reflected Heaven;
In touching tones the simple record speaks
The fondness of a heart by anguish riven.
Methinks hot tears bestream his haggard cheeks
As memory mirrors her loved form to view,
And all her tender ministrations pour
In recollections soft as evening dew.
The well-known voice, now hushed for evermore,
Has left its echoes sighing through his heart;
And as her faith and tranquil virtues rose

To vision clear, he sought but to impart
A brief epitome, that should disclose
All that she was to him, when on her scroll
This record he inscribed, that all might know
That she was one "most perfect human soul"
Whose name in fragrance marks the "town below."

   When gloomy night her sable mantle spreads,
And storm-winds fill the seaman's heart with fear,
The light-house pours its placid ray and sheds
A soft effulgence on this tribute dear.
The keeper's cottage, nestling low between
The light-house and the sombre monument,
Shares the mild radiance that o'erspreads a scene
Whose light appears with mystic shadows blent.

      What sober thought may Faith's clear eye perceive
      With Fancy's pictures fair to interweave?
      Light from above reveals the rocks and shoals
      Whose earth-born flashes shipwreck storm-tost souls;
      Light from above illumes the smiling home;
      Light from above irradiates the tomb;
      Light from above with sympathetic glow
      O'ergilds the memories of our deepest woe.

William Selwyn.

PORT ELIZABETH, 30*th November* 1885.

"*IN MEMORIAM.*"

THE REV. R. TEMPLETON, WHO DIED IN THE ZUURBERG FOREST, JANUARY 1886.

By winding paths, amid the tangled woods
  That skirt the silent deep-kloofed Zuurberg hill,
  A lately wedded pair meandering, fill
Their cup of tender joy. The peace that broods

O'er Nature's tranquil face reflected shines
From loving eyes, as they in converse sweet
Plot out a rose-fringed path with prudence meet,
And mark with glowing hearts its "pleasant lines."
Mysterious are Thy ways, great King of saints!
In sudden fear they vainly strive to thread
Their homeward track, when lo! the husband faints.
Deaf to her voice, with agonizing dread
She dares the maze, in search of human aid.
In vain! The Teacher "sleepeth" in the shade.

William Selwyn.

PORT ELIZABETH, 25*th Jan.* 1886.

"LORD! WHAT IS MAN THAT THOU ART MINDFUL OF HIM!"

PANTING climbers to some barren height;
Eager chasers of some phantom light;
Emmets piling wayside domes of clay,
That, crushed to dust, the whirlwind sweeps away;
   Toilers vain, O Lord, are we.

Fluttering night-birds dazzled by the day;
Wayworn travellers who have lost their way;
Miners groping slowly in the gloom;
Children sobbing round a mother's tomb;
   Blind and helpless, Lord, are we.

Flow'rets drooping in the noon-tide sun;
Autumn leaves descending one by one;
Bubbles dancing on life's foaming wave;
Shadowy spirits hurrying to the grave;
   Frail and fleeting, Lord, are we.

Trembling sparklets of immortal fire;
Infant songsters 'mid an angel choir;
Tiny parts of one complex machine
Guided by an architect unseen.
    None unnoticed, Lord, by Thee.

Dewdrops glistening in a radiant love;
Diamond sand-grains registered above;
Separate nurslings of a Father's care,
That gently numbers every silken hair,
    Weak and faithless though we be.

William Selwyn.

January 1886.

THE RHYME OF THE OX-WAGON.

(A MODEST PENDANT TO PRINGLE'S "AFAR IN THE DESERT.")

Away with the cynic, who ceaselessly sighs
For some new-fangled bauble—some novel surprise
Give me the heart that with generous glow
Lights up the friendships of long long ago.
Green be the mem'ries of pleasure gone by,
When youth filled the cup, and no care breathed a sigh.
Fain would I weave into light-tripping rhyme
The frolicsome joys of the good olden time,
Ere our evergreen forests and still wilds were scared
 By the ear-piercing screech of the Railway Dragon.
And a thousand long miles were triumphantly dared
 'Neath the cosy white tent of a good Ox-wagon

THE RHYME OF THE OX-WAGON.

How jocund the shout of the old driver, Jan,
With his grimy felt hat, and his jacket of tan.
The crack of his whip waking echoes around,
While the startled bush-buck clears the path with a bound.
As the tall forest trees bend their heads 'neath the breeze,
So our team breasts the steep with a labouring wheeze;
Then down the long slope in a sinuous race,
They scamper along at a bullock's best pace;
Wo-haa! shouts the driver. Wo-haa! for the sake
   Of the small Tottie leader with scarcely a rag on,
Who capers and hoots, gamely striving to break
   The headlong descent of the good Ox-wagon.

How grateful the halt near the bush-margined stream,
Where "uitspanned," our hungry and sweltering team
Lave their hot dusty hoofs, and with heads bending low,
Drink the nectar that Adam imbibed long ago.
Old Jan and the Tot gather sticks for a fire,
To prepare the hot coffee (what liquor ranks higher?),
And the lush "carbonatje," whose tender delight
To the palate still clings, though you've dainties in sight;
With biscuits and "biltong" we finish our feast—
   (Perhaps we may take a small sip from the flagon)—
Then join in the chase of a runaway beast
   Who freedom prefers to the good Ox-wagon.

The "inspanning" finished, Jack shoulders his rifle;
His longing for venison all gentle thoughts stifle.
Peeping Bob is intent upon catching things horrid;
While Bill, who confesses to sympathies florid,
Gathers trophies galore of old Cape's blossomed splendour,
While a grateful thought leaps to the bountiful Sender.

Such our innocent joys while our caravan rumbles
At three miles an hour, to the trysting at "Bumble's."
Fain would I tell of our jollity there,
   But time gently warns me to tackle the drag on,
So I leave you to picture our sumptuous fare
   While we drank, "Happy days with a good Ox-wagon."

Well! what have we gained by our *steaming* hot hurry,
But time-tables, tariffs, debts, drivings, and worry?
We've dropped half an hour by a trick that looks dirty:
Old five o'clock reads as the modern "four-thirty."
On a "sliding scale" lately we've slid fast enough,
   Though the "ways" of that slide have been terribly rough.
Dame Fortune has stripped many a home of its charms,
Devoured our profits, and mortgaged our farms.
Our wool, wine, and wisdom are not in "high feather;"
   But up with the whip-stick! Bend Hope's sunny flag on;
"Give a long pull, a strong pull, a pull altogether,"
   And cheers shall yet ring from the old Cape wagon.

William Selwyn.

PORT ELIZABETH, 20*th March* 1886.

THE CAPE OF GOOD HOPE.

A PATRIOTIC SONG.

LAND of serene and sunny skies,—
   Land of the lion and fleet gazelle;
Land where the summer never dies,
   Cape of Good Hope, we love the well.

Land where the birds, in gorgeous plume,
  Flit through the bush or their love song tell;
Land where the flowers show Eden's bloom,
  Cape of Good Hope, we love thee well.

Land where the hunter scours the plains,
  Free as a bird o'er the ocean's swell;
Land of kind nature's soothing strains,
  Cape of Good Hope, we love thee well.

Land where the grape and the orange grow
  Deep in yon cool sequestered dell;
Land of the melon's luscious flow,
  Cape of Good Hope, we love thee well.

Land where the fields of golden grain,
  Rich in their bounteous fruitage swell;
Land of sleek herds in lengthened train,
  Cape of Good Hope, we love thee well.

Land of a stalwart yeoman race,—
  Stern, but with hearts as true as a bell;
Homely, but full of a kindly grace,
  Cape of Good Hope, we love thee well.

Land of the dark Amakosa tall,
  Seeking release from the savage spell;
Land where there's room and to spare for all,
  Cape of Good Hope, we love thee well.

Land of Good Hope! our prayer we raise,—
  May peace and plenty with thee dwell;
Filling our hearts with grateful praise,
  For this bright land we love so well.

W. Selwyn.

THE ERYTHRINA TREE.

A CAROL OF THE WOODS.

Bright, glorious Erythrina tree,
Queen of the forests near the sea,
Herald of springtide wild and free,
Thy scarlet blossoms reared on high
Above the woods in beauty lie,
Tinted in russet-purple dye.
While morning beams in laughing glances
Are quivering amongst thy branches
And glowing flow'rs as day advances.

Bright, glorious Erythrina tree,
Queen of the woods beside the sea,
Haunt of the sun-bird and the bee.
'Neath sunny skies they feast for hours,
Quaffing sweet nectar from thy flow'rs,
Whose scarlet petals fall in showers.
On dark and amethystine wing
Flitting from flower to flower they sing
Their joyous songs to thee in spring.
A shower of ringing notes on high
Apparently from out the sky,
Descend to earth all merrily.
While the Cicada's ceaseless strain
From day to day—again, again,
Is heard through forest, dell, and lane,
Thrilling the woods, a wild refrain.

Bright, glorious Erythrina, how
Thy scarlet blossoms clothe each bough,
The "Red man"* of the woods art thou,
With thy broad banner floating free,
Proclaiming "seed time" silently,
To each dark aborigine.
No written calendars have they,
Thy early flow'rs brook no delay,
The season due, for toil all day.
When Kafir maids with hoe in hand,
Off to the fields a cheerful band—
They go to plant umboua † land,
Singing a wild, wild roundelay,
While o'er each pick ‡ the sunbeams play,
Working in time—the livelong day.

Bright, glorious Erythrina tree!
As time flies imperceptibly,
The spring's precursor thou shalt be.
High o'er the forest dark and green,
Thy crown of beauty will be seen,
While sweeping seasons intervene,
And many a field of golden corn
Spread over sloping hill and lawn
Shall ripen on each jocund morn,
And many a brilliant sun-bird's song
Shall echo the lone woods among,
While red-winged Lories pass along,
And from the shadowy depths below,
Their deep-toned notes in cadence flow,

---

* Amakosa Kafirs are called "Red men," as they are coloured with red clay.
† Indian corn.   ‡ Hoe.

As sounding through the woods they go,
Far from the busy world away,
Where, singing, toils the bee all day
'Mid the deep woods where sunbeams play.

Bright, glorious Erythrina tree!
Remote from cities—near the sea
My winged thoughts have flown to thee.
Queen of the woods! I love thee well,
Oh! for a home with thee to dwell
For ever in the forest dell.
From life's stern battle would I hide
By some bright sparkling fountain's side,
Regardless of all time or tide,
Forgotten be the world's wild roar,
The turmoils of her care-worn shore—
Oblivion shield me evermore,
My canopy the sheltering trees,
My dream—the song of birds and bees:
Good-bye to all things—saving these.

M. E. Barber.

GRAHAMSTOWN, *March 9, 1884.*

www.ingramcontent.com/pod-product-compliance
Lightning Source LLC
Chambersburg PA
CBHW031342230426
43670CB00006B/417